CAMBRIDGE LIBRARY COLLECTION

Books of enduring scholarly value

Travel and Exploration

The history of travel writing dates back to the Bible, Caesar, the Vikings and the Crusaders, and its many themes include war, trade, science and recreation. Explorers from Columbus to Cook charted lands not previously visited by Western travellers, and were followed by merchants, missionaries, and colonists, who wrote accounts of their experiences. The development of steam power in the nineteenth century provided opportunities for increasing numbers of 'ordinary' people to travel further, more economically, and more safely, and resulted in great enthusiasm for travel writing among the reading public. Works included in this series range from first-hand descriptions of previously unrecorded places, to literary accounts of the strange habits of foreigners, to examples of the burgeoning numbers of guidebooks produced to satisfy the needs of a new kind of traveller - the tourist.

How the Codex was Found

The Scottish twin sisters Agnes Lewis (1843–1926) and Margaret Gibson (1843–1920) between them spoke modern Greek, Arabic, Hebrew, Persian and Syriac, and were pioneering biblical scholars and explorers at a time when women rarely ventured to foreign lands. The sisters made several journeys to the Monastery of St Catherine on Mount Sinai, and their first two visits there are described in this 1893 publication. Using her sister's journals, Margaret Gibson tells how Agnes discovered a version of the Gospels in Syriac from the fifth century CE. This text is immensely important, being an example of the New Testament written in the eastern branch of Aramaic, the language that Jesus himself spoke. Meanwhile, Margaret Gibson studied other manuscripts in the library and photographed them; the sisters later transcribed and published many of these. Controversy over the circumstances of the discovery led to Margaret publishing this account in 1893.

Cambridge University Press has long been a pioneer in the reissuing of out-of-print titles from its own backlist, producing digital reprints of books that are still sought after by scholars and students but could not be reprinted economically using traditional technology. The Cambridge Library Collection extends this activity to a wider range of books which are still of importance to researchers and professionals, either for the source material they contain, or as landmarks in the history of their academic discipline.

Drawing from the world-renowned collections in the Cambridge University Library, and guided by the advice of experts in each subject area, Cambridge University Press is using state-of-the-art scanning machines in its own Printing House to capture the content of each book selected for inclusion. The files are processed to give a consistently clear, crisp image, and the books finished to the high quality standard for which the Press is recognised around the world. The latest print-on-demand technology ensures that the books will remain available indefinitely, and that orders for single or multiple copies can quickly be supplied.

The Cambridge Library Collection brings back to life books of enduring scholarly value (including out-of-copyright works originally issued by other publishers) across a wide range of disciplines in the humanities and social sciences and in science and technology.

How the Codex was Found

*A Narrative of Two Visits
to Sinai, from Mrs. Lewis's
Journals 1892-1893*

AGNES SMITH LEWIS
EDITED BY
MARGARET DUNLOP GIBSON

CAMBRIDGE
UNIVERSITY PRESS

CAMBRIDGE UNIVERSITY PRESS

Cambridge, New York, Melbourne, Madrid, Cape Town,
Singapore, São Paolo, Delhi, Tokyo, Mexico City

Published in the United States of America by Cambridge University Press, New York

www.cambridge.org
Information on this title: www.cambridge.org/9781108043366

© in this compilation Cambridge University Press 2012

This edition first published 1893
This digitally printed version 2012

ISBN 978-1-108-04336-6 Paperback

HOW THE CODEX WAS FOUND

HOW THE CODEX WAS FOUND

A NARRATIVE OF

TWO VISITS TO SINAI

FROM MRS. LEWIS'S JOURNALS
1892—1893

BY

MARGARET DUNLOP GIBSON

Cambridge
MACMILLAN AND BOWES
1893

CAMBRIDGE

PRINTED BY JONATHAN PALMER

ALEXANDRA STREET

CONTENTS

ILLUSTRATIONS

HOW THE CODEX WAS FOUND

FIRST VISIT TO SINAI

THE narrative of these two journeys is of special interest, because the first one, that made by my twin sister, Mrs. Lewis, and myself, in 1892, led to the discovery of an early and important codex of ancient Syriac gospels, as well as of three other valuable codices of later date; while that made by us this year in company with the late Professor Bensly and his wife, Mr. J. Rendel Harris, and Mr. and Mrs. F. C. Burkitt was undertaken for the purpose of deciphering the precious manuscript to which we have alluded.

Abler pens than mine will write about these Syriac gospels. It is impossible to predict what may be their future influence on theological thought; yet on me devolves the task of telling how the codex was found, having been, to use a scriptural expression, an eye-witness of these things from the beginning. Many inaccurate statements have been made by too hasty writers in our public prints, and it has occurred to me that the best means of removing misconceptions on the subject is to reprint my sister's journal of our trips to Sinai in 1892 and 1893, from the columns of the *Presbyterian Churchman,* which has welcomed the narratives of all her journeys for the last twelve years. A contemporary account written from day to day by the chief actor in any event, however artless and unrestrained in style, is of the first quality in historical value. I will therefore confine myself to filling up the gap between the two journals, and giving a short account of the convent of St. Catherine. Suffice it to say here that only three persons were present when the codex was found in February 1892, viz. Father Galaktéon, the monk-librarian of the convent, Mrs. Lewis, and myself. Two of this trio being completely innocent of Syriac, my sister was practically alone in discovering the codex, though she will never cease to feel grateful to the distinguished scholar who had put her on the track of it.

For many years my sister had been desirous of going to Mount Sinai, simply on account of its hallowed associations, and because my dear husband had visited it before our marriage on his way to Petra. I cannot say that the library or its MSS. were chiefly in her thoughts, but the publication by Mr. J. Rendel Harris in the winter of 1891 of the Apology of Aristides, which he had found there two years previously, renewed her eagerness, and Mr. Harris himself did more than encourage her by vigorously expressing the opinion that something more might be got out of the early Estrangelo MSS. in the convent library, and by his suggestion that she should allow him to teach her the art of photographing such MSS. He even designed a MS. stand for us, in order to avoid the difficulties he had himself experienced; but while we went to Sinai, he went to Jerusalem and Athos. We had a secret consciousness before starting that we were otherwise not badly equipped for the task of finding something valuable, if there were anything valuable to be found.

We had many years previously studied ancient Greek with the modern pronunciation (for which idea, it need hardly be said, we were indebted to our genial friend, Professor John Stuart Blackie), and whilst travelling through Greece we had found our pronunciation invaluable, and had acquired some fluency in the modern idiom. We had been lodged on several occasions in Greek monasteries, and found intercourse with their inmates both pleasant and amusing; we had also occasionally had instructive interviews with dignitaries of the Greek Church, so that we anticipated no difficulty in making friends with the custodians of the library. My sister's book, too, "Glimpses of Greek Life and Scenery," published by Messrs. Hurst and Blackett in 1883, and translated into Greek by Dr. I. Perbanoglos, had won for her the reputation of being a Philhellene among a people who, whatever may be their faults, can never be accused of want of gratitude, as they have shown to my sister in many unexpected ways.

After having studied Arabic and then Hebrew for some years, Mrs. Lewis had not found Syriac at all difficult, and had been instructed in it by the Rev. R. H. Kennett of Queens' College. Mr. Kennett has not yet visited the Highlands, so can hardly be credited with the gift of second sight, yet it is a fact that he said to her one day shortly before she left for Sinai, " Mrs. Lewis, you will be editing a Syriac book one of these days." Little did either of them think what book it was to be.

Without further preface, I will now proceed to introduce Mrs. Lewis's diary for 1892.

I

Towards the end of 1891 my sister, Mrs. James Y. Gibson, and I resolved to carry out our long-cherished plan of visiting the scene of one of the most astonishing miracles recorded in Bible history—a miracle which has hitherto baffled the most determined opponents of the supernatural in history to explain away; the passage of the Israelites through the desert of Arabia, and the spot where a still more impressive event occurred, the secluded mountain-top where the Deity first revealed Himself to mankind as a whole, not simply to the few chosen ones whom He had, from time to time, consecrated to be the exponents of His will to their fellow-men.

Our intentions soon became known to a few of our Cambridge friends, and we were almost overwhelmed by offers of kindly help and suggestions as to how our visit might be made useful. Mr. Rendel Harris, who visited the Convent of St. Catherine in 1889, and there made the happy discovery of the Apology of Aristides, not only insisted on teaching us photography, but lent us his own camera, and accepted with Christian resignation all the little injuries we did to it. As he reported the existence in the convent of some hitherto unpublished Syriac MSS., I began to study the grammar with the help of the accomplished young Syriac Lecturer of Queens' College, whilst another equally enthusiastic scholar, Mr. F. C. Burkitt, was kind enough to teach me how to copy the ancient Estrangelo alphabet.

The Regius Professor of Divinity asked us to collate two tenth-century MSS. of the Septuagint, and the Professor of Geology to bring him a specimen of what is called "granite graphites," a variety where the hornblende has so disintegrated itself from the rest of the stone as, when polished, to present a surface suggestive of being written over in Arabic characters. Sceptics pretend that Moses deceived the children of Israel by showing them a bit of this as the Tables of the Law, but of course this is pure nonsense, for a rock that is common to the whole district of Horeb must have been quite familiar to the Hebrews. So our journey promised to be none the less interesting because we expected to make some scientific profit out of it, and we could afford to laugh at the prediction that, being women, we might possibly be refused admission into a Greek convent. Our only fear was that, being such utter novices in photography, and having got our own camera only two days before we started, we might be quite incapable of doing justice to a unique opportunity.

II

The most impressive sight we saw in Cairo were the royal mummies, which are exhibited in their gorgeously painted coffins, under glass, in the museum. Whatever may be said in the way of discrediting the histories narrated in the Old Testament, it must henceforth be impossible for the most hardened sceptic to deny that the Pharaohs, at least, have existed. The features of Rameses the

Great* are somewhat shrunk in the six years since his body was unswathed, but there are others who look almost like life, notably, Sethi I., his equally great father. It is no exaggeration to say that for days after we looked on that tranquil, good-natured, dark face, we have seen at least a dozen negroes in the street who are exceedingly like him. The very flesh, and the very expression of a man who lived 3000 years ago are thus vividly before us. We spent much time in the American schools, listening to the children's lessons, both English and Arabic. But as our object in coming to Egypt was to prepare for a trip to Sinai, we first engaged a dragoman named Hanna, under Dr. Watson's kind advice, and then sought, through other friends, an introduction to the chief dignitaries of the Greek Church, who have the pastoral

* The Pharaoh whose daughter, it is supposed, found Moses.

care of the monks in St. Catherine's Convent. The Rev. Nasr Odeh, Bishop Blyth's Syrian Missionary to the Cairene Jews, was kind enough to show us his own schools, and then to conduct us to the dwelling of the Patriarch. The Patriarch himself was absent in Alexandria, but we were received by his Vicar, Ignatius, Metropolitan of Libya, with whom we had half-an-hour's conversation in his own tongue. He was extremely gracious, but said that we ought to have addressed ourselves to the Archbishop of Mount Sinai. For this prelate he gave us his visiting-card, and we found him at the convent, where our dragoman had already hired the camels which were to convey us across the desert. The Archbishop gave us a most kind reception, especially after he had read a letter to the monks written for us by the Vice-Chancellor of Cambridge University, and remarked its interesting seal, viz. the open Bible in the centre of a cross guarded by lions. He was surprised to learn that we had a printed catalogue of the Greek MSS. in Sinai, and good-naturedly took it into his head that our object in going there was not only to make some collations of the Septuagint codices, but to further a plan by which the English might be persuaded to pronounce Greek correctly. " We are a poor little nation," he said, " but our language is great, and we are striving to purify it, so that now there is nothing vulgar about it." Both the Metropolitan of Libya and the Archbishop gave us their blessing at parting, wishing us immortality in this world and in the world to come. The latter promised to write to the monks and ask them to give us every facility for our researches in the library— he even promised us immunity from the khamseen winds !

Dr. Watson has nineteen students in his

theological class, and of these nine were to be licensed as preachers on the 3rd of February following, and then sent to work amongst the villages of the Delta. We sat in his lecture-room for two hours, listening to a discussion on the tenth chapter of Romans; and on our last Sunday in Cairo he preached an eloquent sermon to them from the text, "Who is sufficient for these things?"

The railways are very much better managed than they were in 1886. When we arrived at Suez we were much surprised to find that a perfectly new town, named Port Tewfik, had sprung up at the mouth of the canal. We were told that the French engineer carried the canal away from Suez because the governor of that ancient town was pursuing a dog-in-the-manger policy. Suez is therefore dwindling, whilst her young rival thrives. This is surely a warning to ourselves to be careful in choosing our municipal officers, and

also to make our old institutions accommodate
themselves to the wants of the age.

Some of the rulers of this country, British
and native, with whom we had the honour of
conversing, say that the spring of its wealth
has astonished them, and that there is no
limit to the blessings which a decent government can bestow.   We were delighted to
observe the look of thorough contentment in
the faces of the natives, so different from
the scowls we sometimes got in 1886, and
altogether different from the resigned expression of the Algerians, to whom the French
have shown themselves very hard task-
masters.

III

On Thursday, January 28th, we crossed
the Gulf of Suez in a sailing-boat, and landed
on the shores of Asia to find that we must
wait two hours for the arrival of our camels,

who had to cross the canal and pass through a troublesome Custom-house by a pontoon bridge higher up. We amused ourselves during luncheon with the antics of some baggage camels, each of which had a front leg tied up to prevent its wandering. Some hopped about on three legs, whilst others walked on two hind feet and two front knees. One got a good beating on its long neck from its angry master, and filled the air with the thunder of its growls.

The sheikh, who had been presented to us on the previous evening, appeared at half-past one with three dromedaries. He was a mild-looking young man (for the office is hereditary), nearly blind of both eyes, who showed his appreciation of the situation by saying to Hanna, " The ladies command you, and you command us." The feat of mounting having been successfully accomplished, we started across a desolate plain of sand,

following a beaten track which is constantly
being effaced by the wind-blown sand, and,
like other desert routes, is sometimes only to
be discerned by the help of a tiny pile of
stones, placed there by the Bedaween. At
four o'clock we reached a patch of palm-trees
and gardens fenced by low mud walls, clus-
tering round the brackish wells of Ain Mousa,
the spot where Miriam is supposed to have
begun her song of triumph. As we gazed on
the interminable succession of low, sandy
ridges to our left, we could not help thinking
that the host of Israel had some excuse for
grumbling at a leader who was taking them
where no food and no water could be seen.

The Pillar of Cloud was indeed there,
moving along the very path we were traver-
sing; but it must have been as hard for them
to believe in its Almighty grace as it is for
us to trust in our Divine Leader when the
course of this world seems going against us.

He does not always explain His purposes.
But the events which have made this district
immortal in history are now stamped on the
memory of the human race; they were one
of the first lessons taught to mankind by our
Creator: that He is a just God, and a God
in whom we must implicitly trust.

Whilst our tents were being pitched, a
man named Andreas invited us into a tiny
square hut, separate from his house, spread
some matting over the sandy floor, and placed
some cushions on a shelf that we might rest.
He also gave us a cup of Turkish coffee.

Our sleeping tent was most comfortable,
but we had a wakeful night, as the wind was
strong, and we feared it might blow us down.
We rose at half-past six, but the Bedaween
were so slow in getting the camels loaded
that we did not start till a quarter to nine.
Our path ran through the limitless desert,
over very stony ground, where a few tufts of

2

sapless heath or of spiky thorns enticed our
camels to stop and nibble. Sometimes the
ground was sprinkled with flakes of shining
white quartz, suggesting manna. We lunched
on a hillock at one o'clock; then rode for
three hours-and-a-half over a perfectly flat
plain, with now and then a glimpse of the sea
to our right and of interminable sandy mounds
to our left. We often crossed the tracks of
flood torrents, and our Bedaween guides told
us that a month ago this plain was like a lake.
They have had rain four times this winter,
and each time several men with their camels
have been washed into the sea. We reached
our tents at half-past five, just as the sun was
setting. They were pitched on a little stony
eminence surrounded with tufts of shrubs.
The place is called Wady Sadur. The wind
blew fiercely on the tent, but we hoped it
might change with the new moon which was
to appear that night. Next morning we rose

at six, and at half-past seven we started on
foot over a flat expanse of sand, leaving our
men to pack up. At half-past eight our
dragoman, Hanna, overtook us with our
dromedaries, and for five hours we marched
along, glad when an occasional sand hillock
broke the monotony of the landscape, or a
glimpse of the sea, with the blue mountains
of Africa beyond it, made us content that we
were on the safer side, for the hills on which
we were gazing are seldom explored by
Europeans. Our only diversion was an occasional attempt to read a Hebrew psalm, which
though in clear large type, bobbed up and
down in a way that was fatiguing to our eyes.
So we had to be content with listening to the
chatter of our Bedawy escort in a dialect which
was only partially intelligible to us. The
only times when we understood them perfectly
was when they spoke to our Syrian dragoman.
We also encouraged Saleem, my sister's guide,

to imitate the gurgle in the camel's throat. The men themselves were an interesting study. The skin of their bare black legs is hardened by time and dirt into real hard leather, their feet are protected by the thinnest of goat-skin sandals; their clothing consists of a single flowing cotton garment, more or less white, and a black *abbaya* of goat-skin, sewn together with twine, and well patched. Their only signs of luxury are the gay silk *kafiyet* which forms part of their turbans, and the long pipe which they hand to each other by turns, lighting it with the spark from a flint. All carried the most primitive of swords, and Saleem was burdened with a long gun which suggested doubts as to its ability to go off. My guide, A'agi, had made a pet of the seven-year old camel which carried me, ornamenting its pretty brown furry neck with a shell-sewn red collar; sharing with it an occasional bit of maize bread, and pulling for

it choice bits of the dry desert shrubs. At
half-past twelve we dismounted, just where
the ground was getting broken up into little
sand hillocks, and real rock mountains were
coming into view. The sheikh came up with
the baggage camels whilst we were lunching,
and it was here that the first dispute between
us and our dragoman took place.

We had, in our contract with him, reserved
to ourselves the right of choosing the resting
places; and had intimated our intention of
always resting on Sundays. The natural
place to stop that night, after an eight hours'
ride from Wady Sadur, would have been
Wady Amarah, or else Ain Howarah, two
hours further on. Both claim to be the site
of Marah, and in neither is there now water
near the surface, although Ain Howarah has
a little pasturage for camels. I told Hanna
we must stop for the night at one of these
places, as neither of us felt quite well after

our first experiences of camels and wind-shaken tents; we had told him at Cairo that eight hours a day was the utmost we could do; but that, for the camels' comfort, we were willing to ride two hours further on Sunday morning to Wady Ghurundel (Elim), where there was abundance of forage and chalky water. Hanna thereupon deliberately ordered the sheikh to go on straight with both tents and camels to Wady Ghurundel. It was a very arbitrary proceeding, but it was he who had hired the Bedaween, and our only means of bringing him to account for it was by resolving to deduct £2 from the present we intended to give him at the end of the journey. We had unfortunately contracted to pay him a stated sum for the whole trip, and an entire Sunday's rest meant that he would deduct that day's pay from the Bedaween, though he had told us in making our contract that resting days would be charged the same as travelling days. I also heard him tell the sheikh that we wished to stay a day at Elim, on account of our photographing, a statement which I resolved to take my own way of correcting.

Starting at two o'clock, we passed through Wady Wardan (the Valley of Roses) so called, ironically, because its surface is strewn with bits of black flint. The setting sun now showed us the first shadow of a hill that we had yet seen, and the cloud shadows on the desert are wonderful; when you see one you ride on thinking to get into it; then all at once the black thing vanishes, and re-appears further away to the right or left. It was almost dark when we passed the solitary palm-tree of Ain Howarah. We reached Wady Ghurundel at a quarter to seven, our last half-hour being done quite in the dark. This we did not consider at all safe in a country where the path can only be discerned by the foot-prints of those who have gone a few hours before us. How delighted we were to see the glimmer of our tent candles! and how pleased to dismount and wait till Hanna had unrolled our beds, and Khalîl, the cook, had sent us in a cup of black coffee, preparatory to a good dinner extracted out of the flesh-pots of Egypt, which truly we had brought with us!

A little rain fell through the night, and the morning sun awoke our bevy of hens, turkeys, and doves, released from the durance vile of their coops, and wandering over the desert in a vain quest for worms.

A'agi asked me if we had stopped at Ghurundel to photograph, and I replied, "No, the first day of the week is the Lord's Day. If we were at home we should go to church, but as we cannot do so we must keep it sacred from work."

Protestant travellers, who do not speak

Arabic, can never know how much of their influence is lost through the misrepresentations of their dragoman. How much more these primitive people would respect us if we were not so often ashamed of confessing our faith!

Wady Ghurundel is a long valley, filled with a host of little sandy mounds, covered with a shrub like the arbor vitæ, which is much cut down for camp-fires. A few palms, and the stumps of others which have come to an untimely end, reminded us of its ancient glories when it had twelve springs of water, and three-score and ten palm-trees. The Arabs, like the Greeks and Italians, are very wasteful in the matter of their wood. A little careful culture might make the Wady Ghurundel a splendid oasis. But it is no man's business, though at present it is a vital question for the good of all.

We started on Monday morning at half-past seven on foot, Saleem accompanying us to show us the path. I made him thoroughly understand that we had come to this country to see the way by which Neby Mousa led the Israelites ; and that we consider it a figure of how God leads us along the hard path of our earthly life. I told him also why we rested on Sunday, because God told Neby Mousa we were to do so, from the top of Sinai, but that the day was changed because on the first day of the week our Lord the Messiah rose from the dead, with the promise that we too shall rise to be with him in heaven. To all this Saleem assented. The path led all day betwixt limestone hills. We passed through Wady Useit (the rival Elim) with its few plundered palm trees, and soon saw a heap of stones marking the grave of a mare whose owner spurred her to death. Each one of our guides kicked some sand on it with his bare feet, and spat, to show his abhorrence of

the deed.   We lunched under two palm-trees
in Wady Ethal, and photographed them ; we
also administered a quinine pill to A'agi, who
had been unable to eat any breakfast.   A
stranger came and ate with the other men,
helping himself freely from their pots.

It had rained on the previous day in
Wady Tayibeh, for there was a little rill,
whose water, like all in this limestone region,
had become bitter.   We reached the sea-
shore at half-past four, and here Hanna's
camel had a fight with its master, who tugged
and jerked at the rope round its nose.   The
rocks here are very beautiful, showing
alternate layers of yellow and red sand-stone.

We reached our tents at half-past five.

IV

Next morning (Feb. 2nd) we had a long
ride along the sea-shore, and at one time had
to dismount and cross a ridge of limestone

rocks where the camels could barely find a
footing. The white cliffs were very fantastic,
and across the blue waters is the fine
mountain outline of the African shore. At
noon we turned up the Wady Shellal and
lunched beneath a cliff. In the afternoon we
passed several Arab caravans, the leaders of
which greeted our guides, all being of the
same tribe, with great effusion. They would
first call out " Salaam," touching their fore-
heads and breasts, then approaching they
took each other's hands, and laying their
cheeks together made a sound like kissing,
but without their lips actually touching.
They then said, " Rahmet Allahi wa barakathu
ma'ak!"—" The mercy of God and His blessing be with you !" The cliffs became very
fantastic ; they were composed of a black rock
with red sandstone, surmounted by pink granite peaks. The sand was of a pink colour,
and pink granite boulders were strewn about.

At half-past four we found our tent pitched in Wady Buderah. This was in consequence of my having scolded Hanna in the morning, about his making us hasten on so fast; there was light enough left for me to photograph the camp.

We started at a quarter-past seven next morning and walked an hour over a rocky ridge, then rode through defiles betwixt hills of pink granite seamed with trap rocks and sandstone. At half-past eleven we stopped in Wady Mukattab, and photographed inscriptions. These have been already published and deciphered by Professor Euting. They are in an ancient Semitic character, and are chiefly greetings to departed friends, having apparently no historical value.

We started at a quarter-past two and rode betwixt bare craggy, granite mountains into Wady Feiran, with the lofty peak of Jebel Serbal towering before us. We passed a flock of goats, the first animals we had met since leaving Suez, and observed a great variety of light-coloured stones embedded in the ground, probably brought down by the winter rains. My camel ate of a little dry heath, which grows in tufts, but he preferred a thorn with fearful nail-like spikes, and did not disdain wood! We reached our camp in Wady Feiran after the moon and stars were out, and our camels showed they could walk quickly if they liked.

Next morning we walked for half-an-hour till our camels overtook us, and stopped to photograph Hasy-el-Khattatin, a huge fallen boulder, which Arab tradition declares to have been the first rock struck by Moses. It is supposed that the Amalekites had stopped up the rills from springs in the beautiful oasis higher up the valley, so the people murmured when they saw that they could not get water without fighting for it.

At eleven o'clock we reached the little oasis
of El Hesweh, and were pleased to see
palm-trees surrounded by gardens, well and
carefully tended. The Wady then became
overgrown with the torf-shrubs, from which
a yellow gum exudes. Some suppose that
this was the manna, but the quantity that can
be furnished is infinitesimal compared to what
would be required by the thousands of Israel.
A little rill trickled along the sand, so we
stopped beside it for lunch. A girl, closely
veiled, but with lively black eyes, came to see
us. She was acquainted with our escort, and
her husband was one of those whom we had
met in Wady Tayibeh. Her first exclama-
tion was: "Ma feesh hareem?"—"Are these
not women?" She could not grasp the idea
of our going about with uncovered faces.
She did not know her own age, but A'agi
suggested twenty-five. She had been three
years married, and had two children. I

showed her my dear husband's portrait, and also coloured pictures of Cambridge Colleges, but the green turf was quite beyond her comprehension. She was much pleased at being photographed. Her clothes were very dirty, but she wore magnificent bracelets of coral and amber.

We also photographed a hill, which commands an extensive view on both sides just where there is a bend in this longest of Wadies. Here it is supposed that Moses viewed the battle with the Amalekites for access to their springs, whilst Aaron and Hur held up his hands. The mountain-sides are full of caves and niches, once the homes of Anchorites. Soon a gorgeous sight burst on our view, the great oasis of Feiran, a forest of magnificent palm trees, in a narrow Wady, overlooked by the lofty granite peaks of Jebel Serbal, which rise sheer from one side of it. It seemed at once as if we were transported to some luxuriant spot in the heart of Africa. It is identified with the Paran or Rephidim of Exodus. For four miles we rode amongst these trees, all enclosed and tended. We spoke with several people, and observed a little cemetery right amongst the gardens. Graves here were marked simply by a small headstone and a footstone, just picked off the hillside, with no name or inscription, and perhaps a wisp of straw, which may be nibbled by any passing camel. At one place we had to dismount because torf trees, growing under the palms, would not allow of our passage. These trees gradually became less thick, till we were again upon barren sand, and we passed through a narrow way betwixt steep rugged rocks into the little Wady where our tents awaited us.

Next morning we started at seven o'clock, and plucked the first flower we had seen since leaving Ain Mousa. We were photographing

3

two "nawamees" or pre-historic houses,
curious huts of unhewn stone, built without
mortar, and crowned with a roof like a bee-
hive, when we saw a distant funeral procession
of Bedaween. It reached a little cemetery,
and the body was laid in the ground before
we could get our camera adjusted ; but A'agi
told us that not a single prayer was offered
on such occasions, and that the business
would be finished when they had found
stones suitable for putting up. The Towarah
Arabs do not go through any ostentatious
devotions like other Mohammedans, but they
have a formula which they repeat to themselves daily. It is in their salutations to
each other that the Creator's name is chiefly
remembered.

Hanna said that a Bedawee woman does
not wish her husband to get rich, and that
she will actually try little tricks to prevent
his earning too much money ; the reason

being that she fears being supplanted in his affections.

In the afternoon we turned into Wady Djenneh, where we saw a rabbit. Our tents were pitched at the foot of the Nugb Hawa, and there to our great delight we met Dr. Gröte, an Anglo-German missionary to the Bedaween, who had been spending the three months of winter in the convent, and had made good use of the time in exploring its Greek library. He had no tent, but slept on an air bed just on the sand, and ate with his Bedawee escort. He reported that most of the Towarah are simply starving, and very thankful for the doles of bread they get from the convent. He had been trying to persuade the Archbishop to open a school for their children, and had done them a real service by getting the Egyptian Government to release them from a very unnecessary quarantine.*

* This quarantine, unfortunately, is now re-imposed.

No epidemic could well travel from Syria over these barren sands.

Next day we climbed the pass of Nugb Hawa on foot, followed by our dromedaries. Soon the peak of Râs Sufsafeh burst on our view, and we stood on the great plain of Er-Rahah, just before the mountain which burned with fire, where the voice of God was heard in thunder by the multitude beneath.

At length the convent appeared in view, nestling in a narrow valley, surrounded by a walled garden, and overlooked on the one hand by the cliffs of Jebel Mousa, and on the other by a mountain named after two Greek saints, Galaktéon and Epistémé. The convent is a medley of buildings belonging to every epoch since its foundation by Justinian in the fifth century. Strongly built, low-roofed, vaulted passages lead into a court-yard, where modern rooms of mud and plaster open on to wooden galleries. The gradual degeneracy of the occupants might almost be traced in their style of building, run up to suit temporary wants. The outer wall, built as that of a fortress, is the most ancient and imposing.

Whilst our tents were being pitched beside a well of delicious water, amidst the cypresses, olives, and flowering almond trees of the garden, we were received by the Hegoumenos, or Prior, and by Galaktéon the librarian, whose eyes sparkled with sincere pleasure when he read our letter to himself from Mr. Rendel Harris. " The world is not so large after all," he exclaimed, " when we can have real friends in such distant lands."

We had a peep at the outer Library where some of the Greek books are kept ; and then attended the afternoon service in the church. It lasted for two hours. There was some very fine singing, but far too many repetitions of *Hagios o Theos* and *Kyrie Eleison*. It was the last of their services we attended. They chant the liturgy of their church no less than eight times in the twenty-four hours, each monk being required to assist at least twice during the day and twice at night.

V

On Monday, February 8th, we worked for seven hours in the Library, beginning at 9 a.m. The manuscripts are very much scattered; some Greek ones being in the Show Library, and the Arabic partly there and partly in a little room half-way up a dark stair. The Syriac ones, and those supposed to be the most ancient, are partly in this little room, and partly in a dark closet, approached through a room almost as dark. There they repose in two closed boxes, and cannot be seen without a lighted candle. They have at different times been stored in the vaults beneath the convent for safety, when attacks were threatened from the Bedaween. They

were there exposed to damp and then allowed
to dry without any care.   It is a wonder that
the strong parchment and clearly written
letters have in so many cases withstood so
many adverse influences.

Galaktéon gave us every facility for photographing. He spent hours holding books
open for us, or deciphering pages of the
Septuagint. The fact that Englishmen
should be so anxious for a correct version
of the sacred writings as to have sheets of
paper printed on purpose for scholars to
collate them with all the extant manuscripts,
filled the monks with a profound respect for
our nation.   The only drawback to our
comfort was the bitterly cold wind, the
temperature in our tents at night being
below zero, and as there was no glass in the
Library windows, we had some difficulty in
keeping ourselves warm.   This we could only
do by a smart walk out of the narrow Wady,

where the shadows lay so long, into the bright sunshine of the plain, Er-Rahah. But who may describe the beauty of the sunsets, when tall cypresses towered from the glorious masses of white almond trees against a background of bare granite cliffs, all touched with the gold of heaven ; or the moonlight in that silent Wady, so clear and strong, which made the olive boughs look like fairy lace work ; and the ground beneath them, strewn as it was with fallen almond blossoms, gleaming as if snow lay on it, whilst a few upward steps out of the garden revealed a panorama of lofty cliffs, where intense silence brooded ; and our thoughts went forcibly back to the time when they shook and rocked at the touch of the Divine Glory.

It was on Saturday that we climbed the mountain. Whilst preparing to start at seven in the morning, we observed from our tent door that the monks were wending their way

ST. CATHERINE'S CONVENT, MOUNT SINAI.

from the cemetery chapel situated near us, where they had been holding a service, towards the convent. We said, "Good morning" to our particular friends amongst them, and at last, seeing the Hegoumenos, I deemed it courteous to go out and shake hands. He sent me a shower of holy water from the silver vessel he was carrying, and I said, "thank you." He then held up a small silver cross, telling me in Greek to adore it. I stepped back involuntarily, for I was taken by surprise. "Adore it!" exclaimed the Hegoumenos, somewhat peremptorily. A monk who stood behind him remarked, "Her form of worship is different from ours." "Adore it," said the Hegoumenos again. I saw no way out of the difficulty but that of suppressing my predilections. So I kissed the cross and said, "I adore the Saviour, who died upon a cross." Had I done otherwise, I should have thrown the poor Hegoumenos into a state of great perplexity; he would have thought me an atheist, for his intellect was not capable of understanding my notions. But it was a lesson to me never again to approach a Greek ecclesiastic when walking in procession.

A lay brother, clad in a blue frock, accompanied us as a guide. We climbed a very stony path till we reached a spring of delicious water, called "The Fountain of the Shoemaker," because St. Stephen, a cobbler of Alexandria, once dwelt there. Arab tradition makes it the spot where Moses watered the flocks of Jethro his father-in-law. It is an interesting query where these flocks were pastured. A little rain fell and dark clouds gathered about the mountain tops, but they passed off as we reached the little "Chapel of the Bursar." Then we mounted a flight of rock-hewn steps by the old way of pilgrims, and passing under an ancient arch turned back to gaze on a magnificent prospect of bare mountains and desert valleys extending to the horizon. Then we went under another archway and came in sight of a few cypresses near the Chapel of Elijah at the foot of the peak named " Jebel Mousa," the proper name for the mountain range being Horeb in its lower, and Sinai in its upper part. Within the Chapel is a cave, said to be that in which the prophet was fed by ravens. We gazed on the mountain top, and resolved to defer climbing it till another day, and to direct our efforts towards the higher summit of the Râs Sufsafeh, which is supposed to be the Mountain of the Law. We climbed amongst magnificent cliffs, pausing now and then to get a draught of delicious water, or to pick up a fine bit of granite graphites,* till we reached the foot of the highest precipice : then began a very difficult ascent in which

* Which was not the right thing after all.

hands and knees had to be constantly used,
and the ready help of the monk and Hanna
accepted. The monk pulled sprigs of hyssop
for us, and the Bedaween found pretty den-
drolites for the Woodwardian Museum.
Our eyes were much irritated by the dust
thrown off by an ill-smelling plant called
Sphaka, which it was often necessary to grasp
in order to get over some boulder. At length
we reached the foot of the great inaccessible
rock which crowns the summit, a rock which
no human foot has ever rested on, and peering
over a wind-swept ledge had a magnificent
view of the extensive plain of Er-Rahah
beneath us. The monk, who was named
Euphemios, had brought only bread and
cheese for his lunch. The agility which he
had displayed in climbing tempted us to think
that he had the advantage of us flesh-eaters ;
but a glance at his sunken cheeks banished
the thought. He told us that he had been

fifteen years in a tailor's shop in Athens, and
had come to Sinai after the death of his wife,
having no children. He had often attended
Dr. Kalopothakes' services, and received
much instruction from them; this enabled
him to understand exactly what our form of
worship is. Hanna, who is a Roman
Catholic, struck a false note by making a
disparaging remark about Moses, having
probably picked it up from some German travellers. This was no proof of his sense, for
we should certainly not have employed him
to bring us there had we not believed in the
divine mission of Moses.

As I knew there were three roads by
which we might descend, I asked Hanna
three times which of these we were on, saying
we should prefer to return either by the
path we had come up, or by a steeper and
shorter one which led directly to the convent.
Hanna, thereupon, directed Euphemios to

lead us down the very longest way possible, by a path that brought us into a Wady on the side of Jebel Mousa, farthest from the convent, so that we had still five miles to walk over rough stones, in fact, to make a half circuit of Horeb at its base. I was very angry, and scolded Hanna for not consulting me. We were not consoled by being conducted through two little olive gardens belonging to the convent, in other Wadies, nor even by being shown the genuine rock (a big boulder) which Moses struck in anger. I was so tired that I could hardly walk, and long after the moon had risen I was obliged to sit down on stones to rest. We reached our tents at eight o'clock, an Arab coming out with a lamp to meet us. Our excursion had occupied eleven hours, ten of which we had spent in quick walking and climbing over the roughest of rocks and stones—so it may be imagined we lost no time in retiring to rest.

Next morning being Sunday, we were told that a lady and gentleman were about to arrive from Tôr.   Tents were certainly pitched outside of the convent, just where the Wady ed-Deir opens into the plain, Er-Rahah.   So in the cool of the evening we went down to pay our first call.   We found two young North Germans, who said they were a party of four, and had come for the sake of sport, having sailed in a boat which brought them from Suez to Tôr in the space of four days.   Their dragoman was a Polish Jew who had never been in the desert before. They had never imagined that there would be so much difficulty in getting water.   We were, perhaps, too communicative in telling them about our work in the Library, and the Syriac palimpsest of 358 pages which we were photographing.

We found next morning that Galaktéon expected a visit from the whole party, and

asked our leave to bring them into the room
where we were working. " If they come," he
said, "please go on with your work, and do not
begin any conversation." To this we assented,
seeing that silence is the rule in European
reading-rooms. All the monks were greatly
excited, because they had been told that one
of the German party was a Count, a near
relative of the ex-king of Greece. At length
Galaktéon brought the four young men into
the room where we were working ; they were
accompanied by their three servants, and
made themselves intelligible by means of one
of the party speaking ancient Greek, with the
modern pronunciation, as it is now taught in
Germany, and the dragoman speaking
Russian to Galaktéon. When they had left
I was told that the youth from Leipsic wished
to work in the Library next day, and had
asked particularly for the Syriac book I was
transcribing and photographing. I said he

4

might have it for a couple of hours. The Germans sent in the afternoon to ask the monks for a guide to ascend Jebel Catarina. Galaktéon shook with laughter at this proposal to start on an excursion which would require at least twelve hours of daylight, and at length flatly refused to help with it.

Next day after vainly trying to settle a dispute between the Germans and their Bedaween escort, Galaktéon conducted us to see what he believes to be the very rock struck by Moses. It is not a boulder, but a fissure in the rock of the mountain side, from which a little rill of clear cold water still flows, giving sustenance to a few olives and almonds. The place looks as if it had been rent by a blow.

As we walked back, some Bedaween came and appealed to Galaktéon to bring the Germans to reason. He has become quite a judge amongst them, having been for twenty years Bursar of the convent before he became librarian. They come to him even about their quarrels with their wives.

Later in the evening both the Bedaween and the Germans' dragoman appealed to Hanna. The truth was that the travellers had come into the desert quite without money, and the Bedaween, having been often swindled by dragomans, invaribly insist on being paid for their camels beforehand. Hanna declined to lend anything, saying that he could not fulfil his obligations to us if he did, for he required all the money he had to take us home.

The Germans left next morning, Galaktéon having enabled them to do so by lending them £12. They had never returned our call, nor even shown us the slight civility usual in the desert of offering to carry our letters to Suez. We had been longing for news of the outer world, and especially for information as to the health of our beloved Queen, but of this they did not give us the least chance.   Never again can we accept the fiction that our own countrymen are less sociable than Teutons!   The monks were puzzled as to why the Count had never come with his friends into the convent.   When we returned to Suez we ascertained that the existence of that young man was a deliberate fabrication.

We had by this time photographed 110 pages of the Syriac Codex, Book 16, the same in which Mr. Rendel Harris found the Apology of Aristides.   We had also taken the whole of a Syriac palimpsest of 358 pages, into which no eyes but our own had for centuries looked.   Its leaves were mostly all glued together, and the least force used to separate them made them crumble. Some half-dozen of them we held over the steam of the kettle. The writing beneath is red, partly Syriac and partly Greek. The upper writing of this palimpsest bears its own date, A.D. 698 ; * it is all the lives of women saints. The under writing must be some centuries earlier; it is Syriac Gospels, and something in Greek, not yet deciphered. A Palestinian Aramaic MS. of which we photographed four pages, is the second example of its kind known to exist—that in the Vatican Library having been hitherto considered unique. We photographed also specimens of other volumes, and finished our remaining exposures with eighth or ninth century Arabic translations of the New Testament, which we guessed might prove interesting to our friends of the Bible Society. They show that the monks of this convent had at one time a wish to instruct the Bedaween.

* A closer examination shows that it is more probably A.D. 778.

There has evidently been a gradual degeneracy amongst the occupants of this place.

Some of the Greek codices catalogued by
Gardhausen are actually in the handwriting
of priors of the convent, who corresponded in
Arabic (for their letters are there), with the
heads of other monastic houses. Galaktéon
laments greatly that there ever was a defection
of the Arabs to Islam. It seems to us,
however, that this must have occurred, because
priests and monks had neglected the duty of
instructing them in the Scriptures. During the
fifteen centuries that this convent has existed,
prayers have arisen from it night and day, the
liturgy and the sacraments having been con-
tinually repeated. But as for being a centre
of light to the population around, it might
as well never have existed.

This seems to me, though I am open to
correction, to be the inevitable tendency of
what we call "sacramentarianism," *i.e.* attention

to a ceremonial worship which leaves neither
time nor energy for the instruction of the
multitude.

My sister looked at it in a different light.
" The lesson we may learn here," she said,
" is that our ritualists are not up to the mark.
The Greek Church, which they imitate, cele-
brates its liturgy eight times in the twenty-
four hours, and insists on a fast which they
cannot approach to.   We must tell them
about it."

The Lenten fast began on March 5th, and
all the nice little conversations and occasional
merriment we had had in the library ceased.
We worked indeed, and the monks helped us
as heretofore, but they looked sleepy, useless,
and miserable. Galaktéon seemed very much
puzzled as to how we could reconcile neglect
of what he thought a plain duty with sincere
faith.   I tried to set his mind at rest by
writing after our names in the visitors' book :

" There are diversities of administration, but the same Spirit."

The day before our departure we inspected the church, which is full of ancient and costly silver candelabra. In the apse is the shrine of St. Catherine, of white Greek marble. Beside it are two very costly shrines covered with silver and jewels, sent by the two Empresses Catherine of Russia, to hold their patron saint's remains. But the monks keep these in their original resting-place. Below this is the chapel of the Burning Bush, whose site was discovered by the Empress Helena in A.D. 530, with the help of Arab tradition. The apse has a roof of the richest and best-preserved mosaic we have ever seen. One would rather see the rock. We then inspected a little psalter, which contains all the 150 Psalms on twelve pages, faultlessly written. Galaktéon explained that the monastery had got into the habit of feeding a number of

Bedaween, and must continue to do so, although it is getting very poor owing to the loss of its landed property in Roumania and Russia. On the last evening of our stay the Bursar, the Holy Deacon Nicodemus, took us round the gardens, which he called "the only consolation of the monks," and where blooming almonds and olives sheltered beds of beans and onions.

We left the convent on Tuesday morning, March 8th. We walked for an hour to the junction of Wady ed-Dayr with Wady esh-Sheikh, thus striking into a different route from that by which we had journeyed from Suez. At a quarter-past eleven we found a beautiful shady niche in a rock to take luncheon in. Here we had a tussle with Hanna, who was most unwilling to let us escape the noontide heat by resting until three o'clock. We had previously resisted his attempt to make us start two days later, and thus force ourselves to do the journey in six-and-a-half days instead of the usual eight-and-a-half. It was all to put an additional four pounds in his own pocket. We rode till half-past five and then walked an hour longer, for my back felt as if it were broken with jolting on a saddle which would never keep straight. We got a fright by Hanna tumbling over the back of his camel as he was dismounting. He had been in too great a hurry to wait till the camel had finished kneeling. There were fifty Beda-ween encamped round our tents, and very picturesque they looked in the brilliant moon-light. We were greatly edified by listening to a furious quarrel betwixt Hanna and the Sheikh Mohammed. We learnt for certain, what we had before suspected, that an inferior animal had been supplied to me, and that Hanna had not troubled himself to inspect either dromedaries or saddles before leaving the convent.

We started at half-past six next morning
and walked for an hour along Wady esh-
Sheikh.   Before noon my saddle became so
uncomfortable that I dismounted and insisted
on exchanging camels with Hanna.   He had
not been on my camel a few minutes when he
discovered that the two horns of the saddle
were not in a line with each other, and that
no adjustment of packages would make the
rider comfortable ; so he took care never to
mount that camel again.

We lunched in Wady Suleif, and I had an
altercation with Hanna, who declared that
the Bedaween would not allow me to keep to
the easy-paced animal which I had taken
from him, and which had carried him from
Suez to Sinai.   At half-past five we found
our tents pitched in Wady Igne, though I
had told Hanna that we particularly wished
to make a long day of it, so as to spend the
noon of next day photographing at Sarabit el-

Khadim. We told him that the tents must be taken up and the camels reloaded; then we walked along in the bright moonlight, trusting that they would follow us. At length we espied an old Bedawy racing after us. He told us we were getting off the track, and that the path for a long distance would be across a mountain-ridge, over stones, where a tent could not be pitched. We agreed to encamp at the foot of this ridge; but up came Hanna and said the old Bedawy was telling lies. He persuaded us to cross the ridge in the moon-light. My sister walked the whole way, as she would not trust a camel's feet on the loose, rough stones; but I mounted wherever there was an ascent. At eight o'clock all our baggage camels passed us, both the cook and the Bedaween greeting us with "*Kwaiss kiddi !*"—"This is lovely!"

At length Hanna made them stop, and our sleeping tent was pitched with much difficulty by its cords being weighted with stones—not as usual by staves driven into the ground. After it was fixed, a string of laden camels came against a rope which was in shadow and knocked it down. The roof of the tent collapsed, Hanna being inside, and bobbed up and down as he was trying to set it up again. The Bedaween cut the scanty brush-wood for their fires and for their camels' supper, and as our dinner was cooked in the moonlight, about nine p.m., a more weird scene could hardly be imagined. Amidst all this discomfort the patient good-will of the Bedaween was remarkable.

We rose next morning at daybreak and walked down the stony, narrow valley, whose sides were dotted with bunches of pale green plants up to the hill-tops, whilst its bed sheltered plenty of the white-flowering torf, which resembles broom. When the camels came up we had to insist on my saddle being transferred to the one I preferred riding. Hanna stormed at the Bedaween, though we believed this to be the outcome of his own management; and he stormed still more when he found that the camera had been left behind. On emerging from this narrow valley our path lay across deep white sand for five hours, until we dismounted at the foot of a stony precipice. Here my sister found that her foot, which had been swollen since the day she climbed Râs Sufsafeh, had got a wound on the rough stones, and was so painful that she could not walk. This was awkward, for the descent to Sarabit el-Khadim was too steep and rugged to be altogether safe for camel-riding. Yet Hanna at first hurried on, leaving us without a guide, and it was only my shouts which brought a Bedawy to our assistance. We made my sister remount, and under the shadow of a rock, which seemed once to have been a colossal statue, we found that

her heel was badly hurt. All remains of
ancient grandeur are here in the very last
stage of decay, statues whose outlines can
only be guessed, and inscriptions being fast
assimilated by wind-blown sand to the surface
of their native rock. I took two photographs
of the very confused and extensive ruins, and
was thoroughly glad to reach our tents in the
Wady Suwig.

Our tents were pitched on Saturday night
in the Wady Ghurundel. They were fastened
to trees, and I slept fearlessly in spite of the
high winds. But after midnight I was awoke
by a strong gust, and found the canvas wall
beside me was being lifted from the ground,
with every prospect of the pole falling on my
sister's side, and we ourselves being left without shelter in the bright moonlight. I held
down the rod next me as well as I could,
whilst my screams awoke the Bedaween, and
brought my sister to help me. The former

came running at once, and for ten minutes they were tugging hard against the wind, shouting to each other and to us, whom they could not see. They at length told us we were quite secure, and we went to sleep again.

Next morning we saw the one well which now remains at Elim, a mere hole dug in the sand, where the water sometimes runs very low. In the afternoon we were cheered by the arrival of three travellers, the Rev. Dr. MacCallum, of Glasgow, and Messrs. Morrow and Small, of Philadelphia. The latter were friends of Mr. Rendel Harris, they had come on from Wady Sadur, because their tents were nearly blown down, and they thought these would be safer fastened to the trees of Elim. They were the first who gave us news from Europe since we had left Suez two months previously, and we, of course, took charge of their letters. My sister was poulticing her heel daily, and these gentlemen strongly advised her not to walk with it.

The next two days were spent in a dreary journey over sandy plains, where we suffered greatly both from heat and thirst. As no rock, with its welcome shade, was to be expected, we insisted on the kitchen tent being taken and pitched for us during our mid-day rest. Even within it we became covered with wind-blown sand. My sister rode without a shoe, and several times told me that there was something always knocking against her wounded heel. At one time it would be the stalks of a bunch of thorny plants which the Arabs had slung on to her camel for its supper, at another time a water-bottle. We were at our wit's end to get anything drinkable. Sucking at the little filter became well nigh hopeless, Hanna being of opinion that the very dirtiest water he could find was the thing to supply it with,

5

and it naturally rebelled against such treatment. Khalîl became very ill with the effects of the unfiltered water, which, in this limestone district, contains a strong infusion of Epsom salts. On the night that we encamped between Elim and Wady Sadur he had a furious quarrel with Hanna, who threatened to deduct something from his wages if he were unable to do the washing-up after dinner; whereupon Khalîl shouted, "*Anta Jehûda!*"—"Thou art a Jew!" We were surprised at the expression, for the Jews are known to be very kind to their suffering brethren, and it was passing strange to hear the children of the bond-woman use the name of the free woman's children as a term of reproach.

Our last encampment was betwixt Wady Sadur and Ain Mousa. The wind blew straight on us over the sandy plains from the sea, which was about two miles distant;

it shook the tent, and even shook my bed
all night. There were no trees to fasten
us to, but the Arabs carried our tent ropes
beneath the ground before fastening them to
the stakes.

Next day, at half-past ten, the Bedaween
raised a shout of triumph, almost equal to
Miriam's, as the crest of a sandy ridge brought
us a fine view of the oasis of Ain Mousa,
with a glimpse of the Gulf of Suez on the
horizon. They almost ran, and so did the
camels, and we were consequently well shaken
before being deposited (and photographed by
my sister) beneath some stately palm trees.
In vain Hanna brought me another pot of
filthy, sandy water. I dashed it on the
ground, and a Bedawy, seizing it up, returned
in a few moments with some clear but treach-
erous fluid, which my little filter was graciously
pleased to accept, and return as a wholesome
beverage. I then negotiated with our men

for the purchase of their sandals. It required a little tact, for one of them told me he would as soon part with his eyes ; doubtless, because he did not wish to return barefoot to Sinai. The sandals were only a rough piece of goat-skin cut to fit the sole of the foot, and held on to it only by a projection which is passed between the first and second toes. We re-crossed to Suez the same evening in a sailing boat, and thirty-six hours after embarked for Marseilles on the Messageries steamer, *Saghalien*, having taken a regretful farewell of our Bedawy escort, of Khalîl, and even of Hanna, whose little tricks we might possibly not have found out so readily if we had not understood Arabic, or had lacked the power of getting information from the monks.

My sister suffered greatly from the injury to her heel on the way home, and this led gradually on to a serious illness. We learned to appreciate the full meaning of one of the blessings which God bestowed upon the Israelites during their forty years' wanderings in a region where the strongest English-made boots soon give way on the rough granite stones: "Thy raiment waxed not old upon thee, neither did thy foot swell these forty years." "I have led you forty years in the wilderness," said Moses. "Your clothes are not waxen old upon you, and thy shoe is not waxen old upon thy foot."

IDENTIFICATION OF THE CODEX

THE reader will see from the preceding pages that we came home laden with treasure in the shape of a thousand undeveloped photographs. We were not a little nervous on passing through custom-houses, lest some over-zealous official should mistake our photographic rolls for quids of tobacco, and let in a ray of light before we could do anything to prevent it. Happily this danger did not occur, and we landed our freight in Cambridge undisturbed. We set about developing the negatives ourselves, and succeeded with them beyond what our inexperience justified. A curious circumstance deserves to be noticed. While Mrs. Lewis was photographing the palimpsest from day to day at Sinai, and I was holding the heavy volume on the stand and turning its leaves for her, a task in which Galaktéon often helped me, it happened one day that I lost my place, and so caused her to take duplicates of about thirty of its pages. As we were developing our films at home, and consulting all our friends who had any experience in the matter, one of the latter advised us strongly to send a roll or two to a professional photographer to be developed, in order that we might have a standard to work up to. We sent one roll of the palimpsest and half a roll of scenery (the roll contains 24 films). They came home much fainter than those we had developed ourselves, so faint indeed, that few of the films could be printed from, and thus about 24 pages of our palimpsest seemed irretrievably lost, and we were greatly distressed.

What was our delight as we went on with
our developing, to find that, owing to my
mistake at Sinai, we had good duplicates of
them all!

Perhaps I had better pause here, and
explain to the uninitiated what a palimpsest
is.   In the days when papyrus had become
scarce, and paper was not yet invented, the
old monks used to write on vellum, *i.e.* finely-
prepared skins of animals.   Occasionally,
especially in out-of-the-way places like Mount
Sinai, vellum also became scarce, but the
literary ardour of the brethren was not to be
restrained by such a contemptible difficulty,
so the existing writing on the already-used
vellum was carefully erased and scraped with
knife or pumice-stone; and when this had
been done to the scribe's satisfaction, he
proceeded to use it again for his immediate
purpose, and to write on it something wholly
different, with no regard, or less than no

regard, to the probably far more valuable script that lay beneath his pen. There is nothing that does not leave its mark, however, in this serious world of ours, and it is happily possible often to see traces of the earlier or under-writing on the margins and between the lines of the later or upper writing. Such a manuscript is called a palimpsest.

When our thousand photographs were all developed, and prints made from them, our next task, and that a very troublesome one, was to arrange them all in proper order. My sister took charge of all the Syriac films, leaving the Arabic ones to me. I own to having had very hard work with mine, having to find out in each photograph what passage of Scripture it represented, and get them all into sequence, as well as their tender negatives, in time to exhibit a codex of the four Gospels and another of four Epistles at the Ninth International Congress of

Orientalists, which was held in London in September 1892. Before that time came our labours had been more than rewarded by the decipherment of a little bit of the under-writing of our precious palimpsest. It is not a little amusing now to look back, and think of how nearly several eminent Syriac scholars amongst our friends just managed to miss discovering its value. My sister, when at Sinai, was aware that this under-writing was the Gospels in ancient Syriac, at least the Synoptic gospels, for had she not seen ' Evangelion,' ' Mathi,' ' Marcus,' and ' Luca ' on its pages, and recognised similar words in the photographs as she was arranging them ? I may here mention that arranging was for her a still harder task than it was for me. I could find what each of my Arabic photographs was with the help of a concordance ; but she had nothing to guide her but the top lines of the pages which she had copied from the MS. at Sinai, and these top-lines were often blurred by the under-writing, or even altogether absent from the photographs.   To go over 360 lines for each photograph could not but take up a great deal of her time, and was very trying to her patience.   It required, too, the greatest care and attention to keep all that mass of material in order, and not mix up films already printed from with those as yet strangers to the printing frame.

My sister told several of her friends of the work she was doing, and that she was reading the upper writing, that it consisted of the lives of female saints, and that she had copied its date from the MS. at Sinai, and calculated it to be A.D. 698.   Closer inspection this year has convinced her that it is nearly a century later, but even this is considered surprisingly early for a palimpsest.   It was natural, that, convinced as she was that she had got in her hands a fac-simile of ancient Syriac Gospels,

she should long to know precisely what
version it was, and what its exact value.

It was one day in July that Mr. and Mrs.
F. C. Burkitt were lunching with us. After
all our guests had gone but they and Miss
Mary Kingsley, my sister spread out her
photographs on the piano for Mr. Burkitt to
look at. She told him what the upper writing
was, and that the under-writing was Syriac
Gospels, which she hoped with his keen young
eyes, he might be able to decipher. He
became at once intensely interested, and asked
if she would entrust some dozen of the photographs to him for a few days. This was on
Friday, and on the following Sunday morning
she received a card from Mrs. Burkitt to say
that her husband was in a state of great excitement, that he had written down a portion of
the palimpsest the previous night (Friday)
and had been to Professor Bensly with it,
and that they had discovered it to be a copy

of the Cureton Syriac.   It was only on the 19th of March last, on the evening before we left Sinai for the second time, that we discovered how Mrs. Burkitt, in her excitement, had not given us a perfectly correct account of the transaction.   We learnt that it was the photographs themselves, and not merely a transcription from them, that Mr. Burkitt had taken to Professor Bensly. The two had deciphered the under-writing together, the older and more experienced scholar being the first to recognise the Cureton Text.   What Mr. Burkitt had really written out at home was only a part of the Greek which follows it, and which is hardly yet identified.

The importance of the discovery was at once apparent.   The text which Dr. Cureton found in 1842 among the MSS. brought from the Nitrian desert nine years previously by Archdeacon Tattam, and deposited in the

British Museum, is recognised as of the
highest value to Biblical scholars and critics,
as it is the earliest version made from the
original. But Cureton's MS. is sadly deficient.
It contains—

> Matthew, from i. 1 to viii. 22.
>   „   from x. 32 to xxiii. 25.
> Mark xvi., from 17 to 20.
> Luke ii. 48 to iii. 16.
>   „   vii. 33 to xv. 21.
>   „   xvii. 24 to xxiv. 44.
> John i. 1 to 42.
>   „   iii. 6 to vii. 37.
>   „   xiv. 10 to 12, 16 to 18, 19 to 23,
>   26 to 29,—

St. Mark's Gospel being present only in its
last four verses, and it is well known that the
last twelve do not occur in the earliest Greek
MSS. Here was a MS. which, even from
the photographs of it, one could see contained
a great deal of St. Mark.

To return to our narrative. The same morning Mr. Burkitt brought a letter from Professor Bensly to himself to show us. This was a request to us to keep the matter secret till once we could get the palimpsest transcribed. We did keep it secret to some extent—at least to the extent of not publishing it, and of telling only a few friends whose advice we were in need of. Professor Bensly himself was so much excited that he forgot an engagement to dinner, and the very next day six of us had resolved to make the journey to Sinai six months later, and had communicated our resolution to each other. It seemed an instinct with us all to wish for the transcription of that manuscript. My sister and I began also to urge on Mr. Rendel Harris the desirability of his accompanying us.

Professor Bensly's new edition of the Cureton text was already advertised. With

true English courage, he volunteered to cross
the desert in spite of his precarious health
and inexperience in camel-riding. It would
be a matter of poignant sorrow to us could
we think that this resolution had cost the
loss of so valuable a life. He came home,
alas! but to die, and the place that once knew
him in Cambridge now knows him no more.
But it was not the desert journey, which he
went through so bravely, that caused this
misfortune. It was at Rome that he afterwards caught the chill which proved so
quickly fatal. The day of each man's death
is fixed by Heaven, and we must bow to
the will of the Almighty, who mercifully
spared his loving widow and ourselves the
unspeakable pain of having to bury him in
the desert sand, as might so easily have
happened. Now his loved remains rest
among those of his relatives till the hour of
the Resurrection, and it must be a consolation

to those who mourn for him that his last energies were spent in so high and holy a service.

We cannot well estimate the loss which we have thus sustained for the edition of our manuscript; nor the still greater loss for the critical text of the Old Syriac version, which it was hoped Professor Bensly would edit from the two manuscripts. We may be allowed to express the wish that this important task may yet be accomplished by a British scholar.

A GREEK DESCRIPTION OF SINAI.

I TRANSLATE the following description of the Convent of St. Catherine from a Greek book entitled—" The Holy Monastery of Sinai," by Perikles Gregoriados, Professor in the Theological School of the Holy Sepulchre (Jerusalem, 1875).*

"In the midst of a dry and parched wilderness there rises up before the eyes of the traveller, wearied by the heat of the sun and the barrenness of the land, a green oasis, refreshing and comforting. In the midst of an almost entire absence of human labour, in the midst of a silence like that of the dead, where there is no living creature and

---

* Ἡ ἱερὰ Μονὴ τοῦ Σινᾶ, ὑπὸ Περικλέους Γρηγοριάδου, καθηγητοῦ ἐν τῇ Θεολογικῇ Σχολῇ τοῦ Κοινοῦ τοῦ Παναγίου Τάφου (ἐν Ἱεροσολύμοις, 1875).

no social intercourse, suddenly there appears a little hearth of industry and a light cooling breeze of life. And above all, in the midst of a land in which otherwise neither the nightingale of the Muses sings the song of civilisation, nor the peaceful trumpet of the Gospel is heard teaching the salvation of the world—there, in the midst of bald mountains and steep rocks, the exiled worship of Greek letters found a home for itself ages ago, and the dove of orthodoxy, flying from the deluge of religious bigotry, built her nest in the loved tabernacles of the Lord. A handful of men, flying from the noisy world, following the mystic voice of the earthquake and the echo of old-world trumpets,* surrounded the awful Mount of God, and pitched their tents in those places where Jehovah in cloud and smoke and thunder and lightning carried out the moral education of ancient Israel, that they might bring their earthly lives as an offering to God, carrying about with them Hellenism and Orthodoxy.

" Barren nature was amazed at their adamantine morals ; the savageness of the aborigines, or of the nomade inhabitants, who were often infuriated against them, was diminished or subdued, and cringed in astonishment at their feet. Emperors

* Exodus xix. 13—19.

honoured their virtue; conquerors were pleased with their tried prudence; popes showed their goodwill; kings and dukes scattered gifts upon them; the great Napoleon, in granting them privileges and honours, was seized by a sweet emotion and a great admiration when he found their house inhabited '*par des hommes instruits et policés au milieu des barbares du désert*'; and above all, crowds of pious and learned men sail the seas and cross the wilderness that they may be witnesses of these things, that they may behold this strange juxtaposition of things so opposite, and reverently visit the hoary monuments which have escaped the deluge of barbarism, and the overturning spade of the centuries. Such is the Monastery of Sinai.

" The sacred historical reasons for such a building existing in this place are, first, the wonderful Bush, which the Hebrew law-giver, Moses, saw burning and not consumed; and secondly, the well where the fair daughters of Jethro watered their father's flocks with trouble. Therefore both these spots were embraced in the great enclosure of Justinian, which was four-square, 245 Parisian feet in length and 204 in breadth. Within this enclosure are likewise the many small and somewhat rotten cells of the fathers, an unsymmetrical number of little

chapels and temples, the historical and miraculous
Ottoman mosque, the time of whose erection is not
accurately known, but which must be much earlier
than A.D. 1381, when we have the first recorded
mention of its existence ; and last, not least, the
most important of all, the splendid Catholic temple,
and the shabby, ill-placed, crumbling rooms which
contain many biblical treasures.   Of these two the
Catholic temple is still in splendid condition, a
proof of imperial piety and magnificence, a fine
and hoary monument, admirable as a work of art,
in the truest and best taste, and in particular a
valuable relic of the Byzantine style in workmanship, but entirely in the midst of a dreary desert,
amid gigantic masses of mountain and towering
rocks, a tender shoot of fragrant rose or slender
lily in a ground bearing thorns and briars.   All the
other parts of this temple are surpassed by the holy
altar, where nature and art, where matter and spirit,
rivalling one another, have produced works in which
a glorious harmony is reflected, most grateful to
the soul of the beholder.

"In this holy temple we must also mention the
three sarcophagi of the Virgin-Martyr, of which the
oldest is marble of exquisite workmanship ; the
other two are silver, one having been sent as a

pious gift by the Empress Catherine the Great, the other being the fruit of Christian subscriptions. Yet the holy remains of the Saint are kept in the first-mentioned.

" Amongst the collections of many books, stowed away in divers rooms, may be found not only many valuable examples in which is developed the mystery of the art of caligraphy, which flourished in an extraordinary manner before Gutenberg's inventions, but also monuments having a great and important influence, on account of their contents, on the spread of ecclesiastical philology. The study of such treasures has a double and a weighty use; for noble souls, taking refuge from time to time in this asylum of solitary meditation and tranquillity, treasured them up in this intellectual oasis of the Sinaitic desert, aided by the philosophic custom of condemning those who had broken the rigidity of monastic rules to make copies of the manuscripts.

" We are all well acquainted with the story of the sacred Codex, called the 'Sinaiticus,' which escaped shipwreck for nearly fifteen centuries, having been safely buried here till these latter days, when Constantine Tischendorf, so expert in sacred palæography, out of the vaults, as he said, brought it to the light, and succeeded in obtaining it for

publication, at the Sinaitic Synod held at Cairo in
1859, from the newly-elected, but not yet consecrated, Archbishop Cyril, Constantine I. having
just died ; he received it nominally for a time (*ad
tempus*), but practically, and in truth, till it should
be finally and eternally given away by the young
Archbishop.*

"Of this venerable relic of so many ages,
written on fine yellow vellum, the overjoyed finder
prepared a splendid fac-simile edition, with the
help of imperial Russian funds—an edition which
he described as 'sufficient as far as possible for
the learned who are curious about such relics, and
worthy of the prince at whose expense it has been
made.' But what a strange impression is caused by
the sight of the original, of which I succeeded in
seeing at Sinai only a few decayed leaves, strangely
separated from the bindings of other books, and
treasured here! Besides this, there are still there
many important vellum MSS. of the Fathers of the
Church, and also writings upon paper of other
learned men, among which I may mention the
valuable MS. of Athanasius Ypsilantes, three only

* Donec in perpetuum datum esse (eum Codicem) Archie-
piscopus collegii nomine significaret. Πρβλ. Τισχενδ. ἐκδ. 1862,
and also *Cahiriner Verhandlungen* and *Das erreichte Ziel.*

out of whose twelve books were published a few years ago by the late learned Sinaite, Germanus the Aphthonides.

"In order to make an exhaustive study of all the Sinaitic books, one would require to know not only the Greek language, but also Slavonic, Syriac, Arabic, and Iberian, in each of which there are valuable manuscripts which awaken the admiration of the masters of learning. Many European students visit the convent every year, but very few of them, or rather none of our scholars, have been able till now, so far as I know, to see and investigate scientifically the Greek books, and especially to examine the various manuscripts of ancient liturgies and other ecclesiastical books ; which, if they were well studied and received the attention they deserve, might throw light on many things, and fill up many blanks in our modern study of liturgiology."

A very full and scholarly catalogue of the Greek books has been made by a Russian Archimandrite named Antoninus ; it remains at the convent, and is much prized by Galakteon, who will never give out a

Greek book without solemnly reading you a
full and particular description of it from the
said catalogue. This catalogue has never
been printed. Gardhausen's catalogue, which
borrows largely from it, is very bald, and gives
no idea of the beauty and interesting contents
of some of the magnificent martyrologies
which I saw on my last visit. But of the
Semitic books there has never till now been
a catalogue made.

The exploit of Tischendorf seems to have
made the monks so suspicious of western
scholars, that they have hitherto refused
permission to anyone to ransack their shelves,
and I therefore felt as if I had accomplished
a daring feat this year, when at Cairo I
persuaded the Archbishop to let me under-
take the task. It so happened that the day
on which this permission was given, was my
own and my sister's birthday. To return to
Gregoriados :

"On account of the want of a proper catalogue
of the library, and of a decent arrangement of the
books, I cannot, unfortunately, tell anything exactly
about their whole number. Therefore it is super-
fluous to say, that the most crying want in this
holy monastery is the building of a proper library,
and the making of an exact list of the books, in
order that these valuable relics may not become
food for moths and other abominations. I call them
relics, because, besides other things, it appears that
at least during the last two centuries not a few of
the books have been taken away, partly through
ignorance, partly through the beneficence of the
monks in more recent times. Thus Lord W.
Turner (*Journal*, London 1820, Vol. II. page 443),
brought away from there to Europe not a few
choice manuscripts, such as one of Hephæstion
about 'Measures,' a Speech of Isocrates, the
three first books of the 'Iliad,' 'Tragedies of
Æschylus,' the 'Medea' of Euripides, the beginning
of 'Hippolytus,' and other similar volumes. And
these disappeared for the most part after the
publication of the great Codex (the Sinaiticus). . .
The cause of their loss was the want of a proper
library and a regular catalogue. Perhaps one of
these two evils will be lessened by the catalogue

which has been made during the last few months
by the learned Archimandrite of the Russian
communion, K. Antoninus, who during a visit to
the convent six years ago spent whole months
working among its books.   The study of this
library offers a profitable field, especially to those
of our scholars who have devoted themselves to
the study and filling up of the pages of our early
history."

These remarks of Gregoriados apply to the
Greek library only, but he seems to have
known little about the Semitic one.   We can
only emphasise his remarks about the
necessity of a suitable room, and we may add,
suitable book-cases, in which such treasures
should be housed.   Gregoriados continues :

History of the Convent

"When, on the one hand, the dawn of Gospel-
preaching began to chase the thick cloud of
idolatry, and on the other hand, frightful storms
and torrents of persecution arose, which bursting
upon cities and villages troubled and frightened the

faithful, then the ardent votaries of the new doctrine
of the Cross, ran, some of them, into the arena
of confession and martyrdom, while others, with-
drawing themselves quietly from the world, fled to
the deserts, seeking there for meditation and peace
of mind. Of all lands Egypt was most distinguished
in this respect, and the Theban deserts could see
in their bosom Paul of Thebes (A.D. 250), the
founder of monastic and anchorite life, and Antony
the Great (261—356), who 'caused the cities to
be deserted and the deserts to be populated,' as
the Church sings in extolling him; on account of
which, the sojourn in these places being dangerous
and adventuresome, the sacred names of Sinai and
Horeb, and the regions around them, drew from
every direction crowds of monks, upon the Mount
of God, upon the holy place of the Mystic Bush, by
the well of the daughters of Jethro, and about the
cave of the awful visions and ecstasies of the
Tishbite.   Thus the deserts of this land were truly
peopled, and thousands of Christians fled into the
asylum which they offered, fearing captivity and
butchery at the hands of the Saracens. This is
testified to, first by Dionysius of Alexandria about
A.D. 205 ; secondly, it is clearly shown by the
miraculous transportation by angels to these

mountains of the body of the Virgin-Martyr
Catherine (A.D. 307), and thirdly, by the visit to
these parts of the Abbot Silvanus, who remained
there and superintended many anchorites; *
fourthly, the narrative of Ammonius the Cenobite
(about A.D. 373) coming from Palestine to Sinai to
worship, and the still more faithful narrative of the
Eparch Neilus (A.D. 390—451), who both relate
frightful massacres and atrocities by the savage
tribes; and above all by the existence of ruins of
old monasteries in many places, and of caves of
hermits, which all testify that in truth many
thousands of anchorites and other Christians had
crowded to these inhospitable regions long before
the time of Justinian. The life and the conduct of
these holy exiles was truly 'an exact study of
death' as says Procopius of Cesaræa of the
Sinaites of his day; for eschewing all evil as much
as was possible to men, cultivating the tree of
ascetic virtue with enthusiasm, they dwelt far from
one another with humility and austerity in the
mountains and caves and holes of this cheerless
land, from which they came down and assembled
every Lord's day in the church, where they cele-

* Tillemont, *Mémoires pour servir à l'histoire eccl.* X.
p. 448. No authority is mentioned for the second proof.

brated the Divine Mysteries and feasted together, the most learned among them imparting instruction to the others. According to tradition and to the testimony of an Arab historian, this church was built over the Holy Bush, round which the Empress-Mother, Helena, raised a tower for the protection of the monks from attack, about which nevertheless we have no other trustworthy historical information.

"But this little colony of saints in the peninsula of Sinai could not so easily find peace and security. For so early as the reign of Diocletian the barbarous tribes of Blemmua laid waste the coast towns and massacred the fathers who dwelt at Raitho (Tor), while on the same day the monks of Sinai were put to death, and everything belonging to them was destroyed without mercy. Even in later times the scourge of such attacks never ceased to trouble the weak anchorites, nor did the rocks of the holy mountain ever cease to be stained with their innocent blood, till nearly the middle of the sixth century, when a new leaf was turned in the history of the Sinai monks, and a new epoch was consecrated under the sway of one of the great Byzantine emperors.

"After the death of Justin I. (518—527) the sceptre of the Byzantine kingdom was taken by his nephew Justinian, who during his long reign greatly raised the dignity of the state, and who was distinguished for unwearied activity and the greatest magnanimity. But what no less than political activity and martial successes adorns and distinguishes the name of the great Justinian among the kings of the earth is his great and wise piety about holy things, and his noble generosity in the erection of philanthropic buildings, especially of convents and churches. Procopius of Cesaræa relates that Justinian the Emperor was asked by a deputation from the monks at Sinai—since they had nothing of what they required, they who were superior to all men—nothing in the way of possessions, nor even what was necessary for their bodies, nor even anything that they could buy in a hurry—to build a church, which he dedicated to the Virgin, so that they might live there in prayer and sacrifice. He did not fear the overthrow of this church from the mountain above, but he feared it from below. For it is impossible for a man to pass the night on the top of the mountain, seeing that constant knockings and other divine noises are heard there at night, astonishing the power and wit of mankind. Before such a clear testimony of a contemporary all doubt is taken away that the present Monastery was built by the Emperor Justinian, and another testimony is to be found in the inscriptions on the beams of the Basilica (the Catholic temple) of which the one on the sixth beam says, '*For the salvation of our pious Emperor Justinian*,' and the one on the seventh, '*For the remembrance of the repose of our late Empress Theodora*.'

"A much clearer and more exact account than that of Procopius is that furnished to us about the building of the Monastery by Eutychus, Patriarch of Alexandria, who flourished in the second half of the ninth century, in the Arab chronicle attributed to him, the original of which is in the Sinai library, but most of which is embodied in Greek in the sacred history of Nektar of Crete (published in 1805) who was afterwards Patriarch of Jerusalem (1661—1669), which has attracted much attention from modern travellers. He relates that the Emperor Justinian, granting the request of the Sinaitic anchorites, commanded the Eparch of Egypt to supply the necessary funds out of the Egyptian taxes, and also himself sent a skilful superintendent of the work. This superintendent laid the foundation of the Monastery upon its present site, on account of its being the easiest spot for the purpose,

and because there was water there, and one did
not hear the echoes and thunderings as one does at
the summit of the mountain.* Besides this, the
Emperor sent to guard the monks a hundred
families, and commanded a hundred more to be
sent from Egypt, and appointed Doulas as their
ruler. The architect was certainly Stephen, as is
testified by the inscription on the thirteenth beam
of the church, which runs thus : ' *O Lord God, who
hast revealed Thyself in this place, save and have
mercy upon Thy servant Stephen, the maker of this
monastery,*' etc.

"We know nothing of the history of Sinai
immediately after this epoch, except that about the
end of the same century the new building was
visited by Antony the Martyr, who found in it
many monks, among whom were three speaking
four languages.

"But about the same time the birth at Mecca of
Mohammed, the reformer of the Arab race, was
destined to give a new turn to the history of Sinai,
as a new people, till then nearly strangers, were
brought into close relationship with it, and carried
the teaching of the new leader amongst the tribes

* The Bedaween hearing this echo, say that the spirit of
Moses descends from Sinai.

of the Nabatæans and Saracens, and to the little guard whom Justinian had sent to protect the colony. This relationship, and the influence of Mohammed and his immediate followers, is not apparently confined to that alone, but assumes a more particular character and a more immediate contact, by means of which the Sinaites were able to survive after the destruction of so many of their companions, and to escape many storms of terrible evil. In the second year of the Hegira (A.D. 624) two Christian leaders attacked some of Mohammed's followers, and put them to flight. On hearing of this the Prophet hastened with more than three thousand warriors, gave battle to these Christian princes, and in conquering them gained his first success in arms. The Christians around the Red Sea having received quickly news of the power of the Apostle of God, ran to pay homage to him and to give their submission, whereupon the prudent Sinaites, understanding the signs of the times, went also and did homage and asked protection for their Monastery. The eloquence of these clever monks was such, that the young Arab conqueror was charmed, and he did not confine himself to showing his friendship and pleasure by word alone, but after a year he came to Sinai in

person, honoured and worshipped the holy
mountain, and commanded all those with him to
revere that sacred place, 'where God revealed to
Moses a thousand and one words.' Then the
monks received him with bows and salutations, and
so gratified him that he gave them the celebrated
Testament as an assurance of everlasting protection.

"The Arabs of the district preserve the tradition
of Mohammed's visit to Sinai, and on the summit
of Jebel Mousa they show the print of his camel's
foot imprinted in the porphyritic granite, and lead
travellers to the place where the beloved of God
sat in judgment. This document (the Testament)
wrought many miracles in the hands of the clever
Sinaite who obtained it. Having built an Ottoman
mosque inside the monastery, he ran here and there
and succeeded often in obtaining from the Moslems
advantages and privileges, not only for himself, but
for all the orthodox clergy and for the religious
observances of our race."

ADMINISTRATION OF THE CONVENT.

"The first point that attracts our attention when
we try to say something about the mechanism
which moves the affairs of the hoary Convent of

the God-trodden mountain, is the strange phenomenon, unusual in ecclesiastical history, the existence in it of a consecrated Archbishopric. Why
should a land uninhabited by man, devoid of a
spiritual flock, yet have a bishop, not to say an
archbishop, while time has brought changes to so
many other lands, both near and far, troubling and
diminishing the elect of the Church, depriving them
of a name, and extinguishing them? We can
account for it only by summing up all the evidence
we have been able to gather, from which it appears
that the seat of the bishopric in these parts was at
Feiran, and this bishopric survived till the middle
of the seventh century, when it was dissolved, and
gave rise to the creation of a new bishopric called
definitely that of Sinai. Therefore we find in later
times an episcopal see in that famous monastery,
always meeting with the care and favour of the
Byzantines in Egypt, by command of the rulers
of Constantinople; and with the removal of its
centre hearth at Feiran the colonies of Christians
around that place gradually ceased. Some have
maintained that Justinian established a bishopric
at Sinai, but even after the time of that emperor no
mention is made of any bishop till after the middle
of the ninth century. From the beginning of the

tenth and onwards we have a continuous chain of
bishops till A.D. 1510, when the throne was vacant
till 1540, and again from 1547 till 1567, from which
time till now there have been seventeen archbishops.
The second of these intervals is very important
(1547—1567), because then the bishopric was dissolved in Egypt by the three assembled Patriarchs
of Alexandria, Antioch, and Jerusalem. The reason
for the dissolution of this archiepiscopal see was
the constant rivalry between the Patriarchs of
Alexandria and Jerusalem about their jurisdiction
at Sinai, especially on the part of the Alexandrian
prelates, who left no stone unturned to lay their
despotic hand on the monastery and episcopate of
Sinai, from which endeavour many scandals arose.

" In short, one who has gone through the history
of this episcopate learns that its order and its origin
in the arrangement of the eastern orthodox hierarchy was one of the most burning and important
phenomena in the history of the Sinai convent.
The question was raised in different ways, and
never once argued according to ecclesiastical
canons ; it had important consequences from time
to time, not only unsettling the welfare of the
convent, but also throwing the whole Church into
convulsions. . . . ·

"Time and the Church have solved the problem of the Archbishop of Sinai's place in relation to the ecclesiastical hierarchy somewhat as follows :

" He is an archbishop, having a canonical descent and relation to the Patriarch of Jerusalem. It follows that the archbishop must

" 1. Be consecrated by his own Patriarch (οἰκείου) canonically and without bribery, otherwise his consecration will be null and void.

" 2. Remember the name of the Patriarch who consecrated him (in his prayers, no doubt).

" 3. Be called Θεοφιλέστατος or Σεβασμιώτατος.

" 4. Be summoned at will by the Holy Patriarch of Jerusalem.

" 5. Not have the right to send pacificals or other synodical letters, nor give letters of absolution.

" And to these the Archbishop of Sinai is bound, by canonical right.

" But the Prelate of Sinai is not only an archbishop, but also abbot of the convent, and on account of that, other important conditions have to be observed :

" 1. Each archbishop is elected by the synod and brotherhood of the Sinaite fathers as their abbot, as his rule is given to him by no one except the community of the monastery.

" 2. He is consecrated afterwards by the Patriarch of Jerusalem simply as bishop, but the independence of the monastery in no way suffers from this relation of the archiepiscopate to the throne of the Holy City.

" 3. The episcopal character of the Sinaitic prelate does not affect the monastery, for he is only abbot of it, and not bishop, as his pastoral staff is stretched out over the country alone. Therefore he has no right to sit on the throne; which stands there that no confusion may exist in things which cannot be confused, and that not even the most zealous bishop may violate the autonomy and independence of the monastery, as some have tried to do. There are in the Church most emphatic commands and decisions on this subject.

" 4. From all this it appears that the archiepiscopate of Sinai has a double character, that in the prelate's appointment there must be co-operation between the convent and Jerusalem, the one electing, the other consecrating. . . . If the monastery wishes to accuse him of a fault, it can only turn to the Patriarch of Jerusalem and the Palestinian synod, to whom it presented him for consecration ; thus, if the worst comes to the worst, and there are cross-accusations for grave faults, and a rupture between

archbishop and monastery, abbot and brotherhood,
the appeal of the accusers is directed canonically
to the Patriarch of Jerusalem, who can punish
according to his judgment, even to the deprivation
of the archbishop, but he cannot deprive the abbot
of the autonomous monastery ; yet canonically he
would be justified in punishing the offending archbishop, also as abbot, if accused by the monastery.
And no other Patriarch has any jurisdiction here.

" Strange to say, beside the Archiepiscopate and
the authoritative Abbacy, there exists also another
powerful force in the monastery of Sinai, the Holy
Syndicate (Σύναξις), which represents in the most
aristocratic way the whole Sinaitic brotherhood,
has the greatest influence in its affairs, directing
and bridling the possibly arbitrary conduct of the
archbishop, and through him and with him regulat-
ing the mechanism of the monastery, both internal
and external. . . . . This syndicate consists of the
leaders among the monastic brethren., Its number
varies, and there are Patriarchal decrees limiting it
to twelve ; the syndics are chosen by the archbishop
and the other members, excepting those who are at
the time Δίκαιος (sub-prior?) Σκευοφύλαξ (warden,
also librarian), and Οἰκονόμος (bursar), who are
always members of this syndicate.

"This Holy Syndicate, being thus formed, is entrusted with all the administration of the monastery.

"All official documents must be countersigned by this syndicate, and be sealed with the great seal of the monastery. (This great seal is circular in shape, and in its middle is represented the bush, the mountain, and the monastery; Moses, Aaron, and St. Catherine, surrounded by the legend, ✠ *The Holy Monastery from the Great Justinian in the holy and God-trodden Mount of Sinai in the year of Christ,* 529 ✠)*

"The Δίκαιος has the place of abbot, as we have said, being the first in the monastery after the archbishop. He has the care of ecclesiastical order, of the good conduct of the fathers, of the entertaining of strangers, of the service and monastic education of novices, fulfilling and lightening in these things the duties of the Holy Syndicate and of the archbishop.

"The Σκευοφύλαξ is entrusted with the keeping of the church in order, the care of the holy relics, etc. He holds his office for life, and must never go far from the monastery.

---

* This seal is stamped on the book from which I am translating, a gift from the Prior to myself.

"The duties of the Οἰκονόμος are to superintend all the victuals of the monastery, submitting from time to time to the syndicate a list of what is necessary, and receiving his commands from it. He manages all the relationships of the monastery, judges all its complicated affairs, punishing and rewarding, engaging camels, guaranteeing the comfort of travellers and pilgrims, commanding the tribes of the Kaphyra, himself providing all means of transport, and in general, superintending every direct and indirect connexion of the monastery with the Bedaween, who refer to him as their leader and judge.

"Besides this private and select syndicate, in special circumstances, when general measures have to be adopted, during the journeys of the archbishop to and from the monastery, in the temporary vacancy of the throne, at the election of a new archbishop, and so forth, a general synod (Σύναξις) of all the brethren is called together, from the humblest monk to the highest archimandrite, who all sign the synodical acts, regulate and legislate, having the whole management of the monastery in their hands.

"The whole synod, besides its duties as described above, has also the duty of preserving its canonical

relations towards the Orthodox Church in general
and the Patriarchate of Jerusalem in particular.
The Patriarchs have the care of it, and in the
treaties is expressly mentioned their obligation to
observe the ritual of the church, of the table and of
the other monastic customs. Such are the com-
plete abstinence from animal food in the monastery,
the prohibition of private meals in the cells, of the
storage of wine, and other such things ; the exact
performance of rites, both daily and at feast-days,
according to the variety of monastic customs, upon
the basis of the ritual of St. Saba as reformed by
the Stoudites, no intercourse being allowed in the
monastery with the outer world, nor voluntary
excursions either to Egypt or within the peninsula ;
and the fulfilment of the duties of service towards
the Altar, and the leavening of bread &c."

ST. SYLVIA OF AQUITAINE

ALTHOUGH we were the first women who
had ever worked in the convent library, we
were by no means the first who have travelled
to Sinai, and established friendly relations
with its monks. During the reign of the
Emperor Theodosius, as is supposed, *i.e.*
between A.D. 385 and 388, St. Sylvia, a native
of Aquitaine, undertook a pilgrimage to the
holy places of the East, and has left behind
her a journal, the beginning of which is
unhappily lost, but which contains a very
faithful description of the scenery around
Sinai, nearly a century before the present
convent was built. She bears witness to the
fact that a community of monks had estab-

lished themselves around the well of Jethro at that early period, and a few quotations from her diary will suffice to show that they were of the same kind and hospitable disposition as we found in their successors of the present day.

"We arrived at a certain place," says Sylvia, "where the mountains betwixt which we were travelling opened out into a huge, wide, and very fair valley,* and beyond this valley there appeared the Mount of God, Sinai. The very spot where the mountains opened is joined to the place in which are the traditions of the murmuring. When we arrived at this spot the guides reminded us of it, saying: 'It is customary for those who come, to offer a prayer here, when the Mount of God is first seen from this place,' and this we did. The distance thence to the Mount of God is about four miles in all, through the valley, which I said was a great one. This is a very extensive valley, lying under the side of the Mount of God, which measures, as far as we could estimate by seeing, or as

* The great plain Er-Rahah.

the people themselves said, in length about 60,000 paces, in breadth about 4000. We had to cross this valley in order to reach the mountain. This is the huge and wide valley in which the children of Israel sojourned in those days, when St. Moses ascended into the Mount of God, and was there forty days and forty nights. This is the valley in which the calf was made; the place is shown to this day, for a great stone stands fixed on the very spot. This therefore is the very same valley at the head of which is the place where St. Moses, whilst feeding the flocks of his father-in-law, was spoken to by God in the Burning Bush. And whereas our path was such that first we had to ascend the Mount of God which here appears, the ascent was better from where we had come, and from thence again we must descend to the head of the valley, that is to where the Bush* was, because the descent from the Mountain of God was better there. It was pleasant therefore when we had seen everything we wished to see, in descending the Mount of God, to come to the place of the Bush, and thus across all the valley itself, which is lengthways, and to return with the

* Where the present monastery stands.

holy men who showed us the different places that
are written about in that selfsame valley, and this
we did.   Therefore as we were coming from that
place, where on the way from Faran* we offered a
prayer, the path was such that we crossed over
that very valley, and thus arrived at the Mount of
God.   As you go round about the mountain it
appears to be one, though when you get within it
there are many ; but the whole is called the Mount
of God, especially the one on whose summit† is the
place where the Glory of God descended, as it is
written ; and it is in the middle of them all ; and
while all these (mountains) that are in the group
are more glorious than I had ever expected to see,
yet the one in the middle, on which the Glory of
God descended, is so much higher than all the
others, that when we approached it, straightway
all these mountains, which had appeared to us
glorious, seemed but as little hills.   It is very
wonderful, and without the grace of God I do
not think it could have been, that whilst the
middle one is higher than all, and is specially
called Sinai, that is, where the Glory of God
descended, nevertheless it cannot be seen unless

---

* Feiran, the ancient Rephidim.   † Jebel Katerina?

you come to its very root before you ascend it;
and after you have accomplished your wish you
will descend thence and look at it from the
opposite side, which before you ascended you
could not have done. But before we arrived at
the Mount of God we knew this from the replies
of the brethren, and when I arrived at the place
I understood it clearly to be so.

"We made our entry into the mountain on a
Sabbath evening, and we arrived at a certain
monastery, where the monks who dwelt there
received us very kindly, showing us every
attention. For there is a church here with a
presbytery, therefore we remained the night,
that very early on the Lord's day we might begin
to climb the different mountains with the presbyter
and the monks who dwelt there, mountains which
are ascended with infinite labour, because you do
not go up them slowly and slowly like a snail, but
straight up you go, as if it were a wall, and you
are obliged to descend each of these mountains till
you get down to the very root of that middle
mountain, which is specially Sinai. And there
with the help of Christ our Lord, aided by the
prayers of the saints who accompanied us, I
accomplished the ascent, and with great labour,

for I was obliged to ascend on foot, as I could not go up in the saddle ; nevertheless this labour was not felt, because the desires I had I saw fulfilled with the help of God. About the fourth hour we arrived at the summit of Sinai, that holy Mount of God where the law was given, and there is the place where the Glory of God descended on the day when the mountain smoked. And in that spot there is now a little church, because the said place, which is the summit of the mountain, is not very large. But nevertheless the church has of itself great grace. When, then, with the help of God we ascended to that summit, and arrived at the door of that church, behold, the presbyter met us, coming from his monastery, which is considered to belong to the church, a healthy old man—a monk of what is called the ascetic life here, one moreover who is worthy to be in this place. Other presbyters also came to meet us, but not all the monks who dwell here close to the mountain, that is, those who are not prevented by weakness or age. But no one dwells at the summit of the middle mountain, for there is nothing else there save only the church and the cave where St. Moses was. Having read in the very place all from the Book of Moses, and having made an offering in

due order, and we having partaken of the communion, just as we were going out of the church
the presbyters of the same place gave us thank-
offerings,* that is, gifts of apples (oranges ?) which
grow in the mountain itself. For, although the
hoary mountain of Sinai is all stony, and has no
corn, nevertheless below, near the root of these
mountains, that is, both about the one in the
middle, and about those that surround it, there
are little rills, and the holy monks plant young
trees diligently about them, and establish little
apple-gardens, or houses of prayer, and near to
them monasteries, so that they gather a little
fruit from the earth of the mountain itself, and
these they cultivate with their own hands.

"Then, after we had communicated, and these
holy men had given us εὐλογίας, and we had gone
out of the door of the church, then I began to
request them to show us the different places ; and
forthwith these holy men deigned to do so, for
they pointed out to us the very cave where St.
Moses was when he ascended the second time into
the Mount of God, that he might receive again the

* Εὐλογίας, just as the monks of the present day gave us
occasionally gifts of dates, pomegranates, delicious quince-
jelly, almonds, and date-brandy.

tablets after he had broken them on account of the
people's sin, and other places, whatever we desired,
or those that they knew better about they deigned
to show us. Egypt also, and Palestine, and the
Red Sea, and the Mare Parthenicum, which reaches
to Alexandria, and also the far-away borders of the
Saracens, we saw below us, as I think was hardly
possible. But all these different things the holy
men declared to us.

"Having then fulfilled every desire which had
impelled us to ascend, we began to descend from
the summit of the Mount of God, and went up to
another mountain,* which is joined to it, and is the
place called Horeb. Here also there is a church,
for this place is Horeb, where St. Elijah the prophet was, to which he fled from the face of King
Ahab, where God spake to him, saying: 'What
doest thou here, Elijah?' as it is written in the
Book of the Kings, for here the cave where St.
Elijah was hid is seen to-day before the door of the
church which is there. A stone altar also is seen,
which St. Elijah himself placed there to sacrifice to
God, as these holy men deigned to show us. We
made an oblation and a long prayer, and read a

* Jebel Mousa.

portion of the Book of Kings. This we desired very much to do always, and wherever we went we always read a portion of the Book about it.

"Having made an offering there, we went immediately to another place not far from it, the presbyters and monks showing us, that is, to the place* where St. Aaron stood with the seventy elders while St. Moses received from God the law for the children of Israel. For in that place, although it has no roof, nevertheless there is a huge rock, having a flat surface on the top, on which these holy men are said to have stood, and in the midst of it they had made an altar of stones. So we read here the very place in the Book of Moses, and repeated a psalm suitable to the spot, and having offered a prayer, we descended thence. It now began to be about the eighth hour, and we had still three miles to go before we could leave the mountain-region that we had entered the night before, but we had not to go out at the same place by which we had made our way, but as I said above, necessity was laid upon us to visit all the holy places and to see all the monasteries that were there, and thus to go out at the head of the

---

* The hill now called by the Arabs Harûn.

valley which I described above, that is, which lies
below the Mount of God.   Therefore it was necessary for us to go out at the head of that valley,
because there were in it many monasteries of holy
men, and a church in the place where the bush is,
the bush that is green to this day, and sends out
shoots.

"We thus went down from the Mount of God,
and arrived at the bush about the tenth hour.   In
front of the church there is a beautiful garden,*
having abundance of fine water, and in this garden
is the bush itself.   Near to it also the place is
shown where St. Moses stood when God said to
him, 'Loose the latchet of thy shoe,' etc., and when
we arrived at this place it was already the tenth
hour, and because it was so late we could not make
an offering.   But prayer was made in the church,
and also near the bush in the garden, and we read
the very place in the Book of Moses, according to
our custom.   And because it was late, we supped
in the garden before the bush with the holy men
themselves, and we encamped there.   And waking
next morning very early, we begged the presbyters
that an offering should be made, and this was done.

.* The very garden in which *our* tents were pitched.

The holy men began to show us the various places as we went away from the bush. They pointed out to us the place where the tents of the children of Israel were in those days, when Moses was in the mountain. They showed us also the place where the calf was made, for a great stone is fixed in that place unto this day. We also as we went saw before us the summit of the mountain that looks down over all the valley, from which place St. Moses saw the children of Israel dancing in those days when they made the calf. They showed us also a great stone in the place where St. Moses descended with Joshua, the son of Nun. Close to this stone he waxed wroth, and broke the tablets which he was carrying. They showed us also in what manner each of them had his dwelling in this valley. The foundations of these dwellings appear to this day as if they were surrounded by stone ; they showed us also the place where St. Moses ordered the children of Israel to run from gate to gate, he returning to the mountain.* Then they showed us the place where the calf was burnt which Aaron had made for them, by order of Moses. Likewise they showed us the stream from which

* Exodus xxxii. 27.

St. Moses gave to drink to the children of Israel,
as it is written in Exodus.   They showed us also
the place where the seventy men received some of
the spirit of Moses.   They showed us also the place
where the children of Israel lusted for food.   They
also pointed out to us the place which is called the
Conflagration, because part of the tents were burnt
there;* then the fire ceased when Moses prayed.
They showed us also the place where manna and
quails rained on them.

  " And thus the various things (which are) written
in the Books of St. Moses as having been done in
this place, namely, this valley, which, as I said,
lies under the Mount of God, the holy Sinai, were
shown to us, which it would be enough if I wrote
them all singly, because no one could retain so
much, but when you read the holy Books of Moses
with devotion, all things are more closely seen
which were done here.   For this is the valley
where the Passover was celebrated when a year
had passed from the departure of the children of
Israel out of the land of Egypt, because in that
valley the children of Israel remained some time,
that is, while St. Moses ascended into the Mount of

* Numbers xi. 3.

God, and descended the first and second times; and again, they remained there for some time while the Tabernacle was being made, and the various things which were shown in the Mount of God. The same day we met with some very holy monks, who on account of their age or imbecility cannot go to the Mount of God to make offerings, but who nevertheless deigned to take us into their monasteries.

"Thus having seen all the holy places which we desired, and all the places where the children of Israel passed going and coming to the Mount of God, having seen also the holy men who dwelt there, we returned to Faran in the name of God. And we ought to give thanks to God in everything, I will not say in so many and such things as He has deigned to confer upon me, an unworthy woman of no merit, that I should walk about all the places of which I was not worthy; nor can I sufficiently thank all those holy men who deigned to take my little self with a willing mind into their monasteries, and lead me about through all those places which I asked about according to the Scriptures. Many also of these holy men themselves, who dwelt in the mountain of God or round about it, deigned to accompany us to Faran, those at least who were stronger in body."

We refer those of our readers who wish to know more of St. Sylvia's diary to the story itself, in the original Latin, by J. F. Gamurrini (Rome, ex typis Vaticanis, 1888). There they will learn how she went to Jerusalem, and witnessed all the ceremonies of Passion Week,—how she heard short sermons from the bishop and from all the presbyters in turn, proving to us that such exhortations were more common in the Greek Church of the fourth century than they are now,—how she went to the burial-place of Job, and also to Haran, to the very spot where Eleazer met with Rebecca.

The whole diary throws a flood of light on the state of Eastern Christendom before the fall of the Roman Empire, and proves that the love of adventure is by no means a new phenomenon in our sex. This fourth-century narrative of a woman's experience, before a stone of the present venerable monastery was

laid, is singularly like our own. Sylvia discovered no manuscripts, for the oldest of
those now existing had then hardly begun to
be written.   She must have carried with her
manuscripts of the Pentateuch and of the
Books of Kings; and she succeeded in seeing
a supposed letter of our Lord to Abgah, King
of Edessa.

A more modern coincidence deserves to
be noted.   For the first two years of our
residence in Cambridge we occupied a semi-
detached house, and were during that time
under the same roof as one of Canon Cureton's
married daughters.   As my sister could not
obtain even a second-hand copy of the Cureton Gospels for love or money, this lady
very kindly lent her her father's own copy,
to take with us on our second visit to Sinai.

The following lines were written by my
sister for her Christmas-card in the winter
of 1892:

Χάρις ἐπὶ Χάριτος

One more year since Christ was like us
    In a tent of clay;
One year less till He shall take us
    Home for aye.
Oh how bright the path before us!
Oh how great the glory o'er us!
Oh how strong the Hand that tore us
    From sin's sway!

One year less of toil and trouble,
    Till we see His face;
Each new step will gain us double
    In our race.
Less and less of tears and sinning,
More and more of work and winning,
Joy that ends in fresh beginning,
    Grace for grace.

SECOND VISIT TO SINAI

(From Mrs. Lewis's Journal)

THE story of our first visit to Sinai in the pages of the *Churchman* for August had scarcely been finished when an event occurred which made us resolve to return thither within six months. Our readers may remember that we described a Syriac palimpsest, of which the later writing is a martyrology and the earlier one the four Gospels. As my eyes are not keen enough to decipher more than a few separated words of the latter, I took several opportunities of showing the photographs to Syriac scholars, with the result that no one thought they could be read, until I placed a few of the clearest ones in the

hands of Mr. F. C. Burkitt. They were
shown by him to Professor Bensly, and the
two identified the version as of the same
type as that discovered by Cureton in 1842,
though with considerable variation in the
readings. It thus appeared that my efforts
had been the means of bringing to light an
early text of the Gospels which would supple-
ment the Curetonian one, and be not without
value for the light it might throw on
disputed passages. A portion of it could
be deciphered from my photographs, but the
rest was only to be seen from the pages of
the manuscript itself. The three gentlemen
who undertook to transcribe it, and amongst
whom I divided some 360 photographs,
Professor Bensly, Mr. Rendel Harris, and
Mr. Burkitt, volunteered to go with my
sister and me on a joint expedition to Sinai,
Mrs. Bensly and Mrs. Burkitt accompanying us.

We spent a few weeks at Cairo, and made three calls on the Archbishop. The first time we went by ourselves, and my sister asked him to allow her to catalogue the Arabic MSS. in the convent. She renewed her request when we again called to introduce Professor and Mrs. Bensly, and again when we went with Mr. and Mrs. Burkitt, adding on the third occasion that we should also like to do the Syriac ones. The result was that he wrote a letter to the monks, telling them that the work of cataloguing was to be in our hands only, and that every facility for examining the books was to be given to the party, on condition that we left for the use of the convent copies of the said catalogues in Greek.

Mr. Rendel Harris met us at Suez, and we went into the desert on the 30th January. Dr. Watson had recommended to us a dragoman who was much superior to the

one we had last year. Though a Moham-
medan, he has always been a *protégé* of
the late Dr. Lansing. We were fanned by
a cooling breeze, and the road seemed less
monotonous than formerly, for it was
enlivened by philological discussions, by
scraps of song, of wit, and of story. We
reached the convent about mid-day on
February 8th, were received at the gate by
the Bursar, Nicodemus, and conducted to
the parlour of Galaktéon the librarian, who
now fills the office of Hegoumenos or Abbot.

He received us with a cordiality that was
almost overpowering, and was directed
chiefly to myself. He hardly knew, in fact,
how to express his delight. He kept me
behind after the others had left, and told
me that he looked on me in the light of his
mother, that he would be guided by my
advice in everything, and that as four of the
party were as yet strangers to him, he would

prefer that all requests for books, etc., should come to him at first through me.

I, of course, assented to this arrangement, and asked if it would be convenient for us to visit the library in the afternoon.

So we returned at the appointed hour, only too anxious to set our eyes again on the dear old palimpsest. No sooner were we seated than the Abbot entered holding up a blood-stained pocket-handkerchief, and displaying behind it a face and head streaming from recent wounds. His tall cap had fallen off, and his long hair hung down in a helpless fashion. He sank groaning into a chair, and exclaimed, " I have fallen, oh, I am suffering." It was evident that he had been roused to receive us, and when only half awake had gone tilt against the door of the tiny dark closet which does duty for his bedroom. Of course we recommended him to retire to rest, and said we would not trouble him about the library till to-morrow, but he was determined to show it to us, so we were obliged to accompany him thither, he resisting all attempts on the part of the monks and ourselves to put a little plaster on his wounds, which, though many, were only skin deep. But we knew that he had had a serious illness since we were last at Sinai, and notwithstanding his pleasant jest about passing himself off as my son should he ever visit England, he appears to be well over sixty. So we were all not a little anxious lest he should have a feverish night, and delay our friends' chance of beginning work on the palimpsest.

Next morning (Friday) he tottered to what is called the Archbishop's room, where the Syriac books are kept, and asked me what we wished to see first. I replied, "All the books which we photographed last year," and as I had anticipated, the palimpsest and

9

the Jerusalem Lectionary were both produced along with some other Syriac books from a cupboard. I at once asked Galaktéon if he would let me have the Lectionary in my tent, as I wished to work at it myself, and if he would let me have the palimpsest to give employment to my friends. "Just as you wish," was the reply. Whilst I was examining these treasures Mr. Rendel Harris held out another "Jerusalem Lectionary," dated four years later than the one I had discovered, *i.e.* in A.D. 1120, and which is thus the third one of its kind extant. I carried both, with the palimpsest, to our tents, and it may be imagined that the latter at once underwent a critical examination.

Mr. Harris pronounced it to be by no means a difficult palimpsest, but the pages varied greatly in distinctness, and though even I could trace the words (being of their natural size) as I could not do in my photographs, there were many from which the actual ink of the under-writing had faded, leaving only faint indications on the vellum from which words could be traced. Add to this that many of these words were covered by the dark upper writing which was happily of a different colour, and that most of it had to be read between the lines, and my readers may appreciate the difficulty of the task which was to be undertaken. However, after much discussion, the three scholars agreed to the following division of labour. Mr. Rendel Harris to read the first hundred and four pages, Mr. Burkitt the second hundred or more (these included thirty which he had already copied from my photographs) and Professor Bensly the remainder, together with revising as much of the others' work as possible. The Gospels were already known to stop after page 320, as the rest of the palimpsest writing treats of other subjects, partly Syriac and partly Greek. The day was to be divided into three watches, so that some one might be always at work from eight o'clock till eleven, from eleven till two, and from two till five. But as there was a deficiency of bright sunlight after half-past three, and this made a considerable difference to such work, each separate watch was taken in turns on successive days. The manuscript lay in my tent at night, Mrs. Bensly having made a pretty silk cover for it, and was fetched out soon after daybreak in order that Professor Bensly might secure an hour's work before the first watch began. Nor did the coming of darkness bring rest to its pages, for I often sat up till half-past ten to copy some story in the upper writing after Professor Bensly had finished with it.

We began our work on the catalogues at once. The monks read their Archbishop's letter, and then said that they would never

have placed all their treasures in the hands
of anyone whom they did not thoroughly
know and trust, but that they would most
willingly comply with my wish that Mr.
Rendel Harris should help me with the
Syriac manuscripts, and that one of themselves should relieve my sister from the
laborious task of counting the pages of the
Arabic ones.

So ten or fifteen volumes were carried up
at a time from the various little closets, which
are called libraries only by courtesy, and from
old chests stored away in the queerest of
corners. They lay on the table so that
Professor Bensly and Mr. Burkitt might
have the opportunity of examining them as
soon as we did, and we spent several hours
and days in the often very monotonous task
of the necessary counting and describing. I
left the copying of titles to Mr. Harris, unless
a volume looked as if it might prove very

interesting, when we searched its pages together.

Mrs. Bensly kindly undertook to count pages for my sister, but the Arabic books so greatly outnumbered the Syriac that the monks also came to her aid, and the little draughty room, with its glassless windows, was sometimes filled with some half-dozen of the holy fathers, counting assiduously under their abbot's directions. They were always greatly pleased when the contents of a book were explained to them. Mr. Harris's thorough knowledge of Church history and of patristic literature proved invaluable in helping us to identify the often strangely sounding and strangely spelt titles of Arabic books.

I had still another project in regard to the palimpsest, which my friends were one and all reluctant to let me disclose, as they did not know how the monks would take it. I had

made enquiries in the manuscript room of
the British Museum as to the best means of
reviving ancient writing, when faded, without
risk of injury either to the script or to
the vellum.   I had come provided with four
bottles of a very ill-scented composition, from
the fumes of which I hoped to be protected
by a respirator specially designed for the
purpose.

For ten days I had to restrain my
impatience about using this, but on the
eleventh I happened to open a large volume
of Mar Isaac's discourses which I had known
on our former visit, and which contained
many pages so faded as to be quite illegible.
I asked Galaktéon to let me restore one of
these, with the result, that it came up in a
brilliant hue of dark green, and he was so
astonished that he asked me to paint up the
whole volume, then to try my " scent bottle,"
as it was called, on other hoary documents.

How triumphant I felt when he gave me
permission to touch up the palimpsest, though
only in places where it could not be read
otherwise. Professor Bensly at first dis-
approved of the proceeding, but as both his
fellow-workers gave my brush the warmest
of welcomes, he was induced after a few days
to ask for it himself, and many a blank
margin thus became covered with very
distinct writing. How many lines were thus
restored to the text we cannot well estimate,
but in Mr. Harris's portion it might perhaps
be a sixth of the whole. Moreover, in
difficult passages I was often able to verify
the words which one of my friends had
deciphered. It was thus that the final
colophon came to light, telling that these
were the "separated Gospels." The next
column probably contains a date, but it
baffled all my efforts to bring up more than
a few words, and is evidently written with

ink which ought to be treated by another chemical.

Mrs. Bensly, besides giving some help to her husband and to my sister, found a sphere of usefulness in trying to teach some Bedawee women to knit. There were two poor creatures who had never known the use of soap and water, who spent most of their time sitting with a couple of children outside the convent gate, and whose home was under a great rock. Their condition was apparently not much above that of the lower animals, and they had had no opportunity of learning anything from one of their own sex. The stupid creatures refused to learn, but some men and boys took up the work so eagerly that their kind teacher could not supply them all with materials.

The three of us who could speak Greek occasionally got into a religious discussion with the monks, especially Nicodemus, who was very anxious to convince us of the good which ascetics had done in the world. "These manuscripts would not be here for you to copy," he would exclaim, "if pious men had not retired into the desert to write them." We thought it wiser not to make the obvious retort, viz. that the monks of the last few centuries had quite failed to comprehend the value of what their predecessors had done. We Presbyterians had rather the advantage over our companions of the Society of Friends and of the Church of England, when we were asked if we accepted the authority of Synods; but we startled Nicodemus by persistently refusing to acknowledge any mediator except the Lord Jesus Christ in our approach to the Father. In discussions with Greek monks, when one gets to a thorny subject, such as the priesthood, a safe plan is to say something about the Pope; this causes a diversion of their energies to an antagonist worth hitting.

The day before our departure a question
of mine induced Galaktéon to take us to the
coal-cellar, and show us a dark prison-hole, or
oubliette, to be entered only by a steep ladder.
I had no wish to blacken myself, but Mr.
Harris went down amidst a shower of fare-
wells in several languages. He found a
succession of secret chambers communicating
with each other, and Galaktéon confessed to
having been once confined there for twenty-
four hours, without food, when he had com-
mitted a breach of monastic order.

Our journey homewards was a remarkably
pleasant one. Heavy showers fell at night,
and cooling winds made our rides over the
waste enjoyable. The only exception to
this was a gust of sand-laden wind which
struck suddenly down on us in the Wady
esh-Scheikh, and a storm of sand into which
we rode between Wady Ghurundel and
Sadur.

On the last night of our desert journey
three of us hurried on to A'yun Mousa after
dinner, that we might be in time to catch the
Marseille boat.   Never shall we forget the
silent glory of the moon-lit sands, and the
ghost-like shadows of the palm trees which
told of our approach to civilisation and rest.
We could only regret that we had hitherto
made no use of these evening hours for
travelling, but it is of course impossible to
move a camp after it has once settled to
the serious business of dining.

It is too soon to tell what the influence
of the newly-found Codex will be upon the
Canon of Scripture.   The last twelve verses
of St. Mark's Gospel are conspicuous by their
absence, St. Luke beginning on the same
page as St. Mark ends.   The greeting of the
angels to the shepherds in Luke ii. 14 is
" Good will towards men."   Lastly, our manu-

script is linked to the Curetonian by its colophon, which came up under the reviver, and which tells us that these are "the separated Gospels." The Gospels end on page 320 of the manuscript; the remainder is apocryphal writings, in Syriac and in Greek, which are as yet only partly transcribed.

We can only hope that this discovery of an early text of God's great message to the world may lead to an increased interest in Syriac studies, and to a renewed search in Eastern monasteries for further documents, which will, like the "Apology of Aristides," give us a more intelligent insight into the lives of the first martyrs and confessors.

THE END

J. PALMER, PRINTER, ALEXANDRA STREET, CAMBRIDGE

www.ingramcontent.com/pod-product-compliance
Ingram Content Group UK Ltd.
Pitfield, Milton Keynes, MK11 3LW, UK
UKHW042152280225
455719UK00001B/282